THE AUDACITY
TO CHANGE!

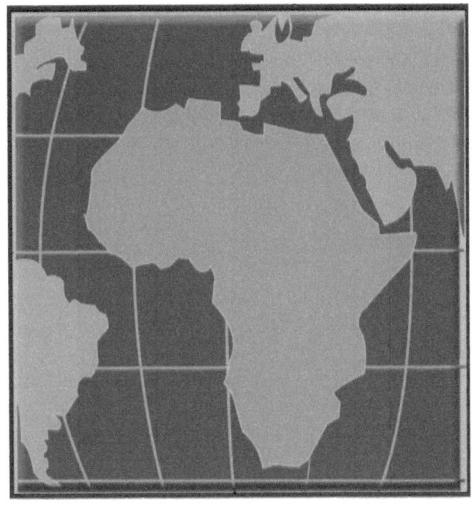

BREAKING THE
BERLIN WALL IN AFRICA

Professor M. D. Kaluya

iUniverse, Inc.
Bloomington

The AUDACITY to CHANGE:
BREAKING the BERLIN WALL in AFRICA

iUniverse books may be ordered through booksellers or by contacting:

iUniverse
1663 Liberty Drive
Bloomington, IN 47403
www.iuniverse.com
1-800-Authors (1-800-288-4677)

Because of the dynamic nature of the Internet, any Web addresses or links contained in this book may have changed since publication and may no longer be valid. The views expressed in this work are solely those of the author and do not necessarily reflect the views of the publisher, and the publisher hereby disclaims any responsibility for them.

Any people depicted in stock imagery provided by Thinkstock are models, and such images are being used for illustrative purposes only.

Certain stock imagery © Thinkstock.

ISBN: 978-1-4502-8577-3 (sc)
ISBN: 978-1-4502-8578-0 (ebk)

Printed in the United States of America

iUniverse rev. date: 01/12/2011

Dedication

This book is dedicated to my mother, Ednance Kagoya, who raised me up with the spirit of wanting to search for knowledge; my father, Sam Isooba, for his moral and material support in my early years; my elder sister, Harriet Mwenze, who is my second mother and picked up the tools from my mother to ensure that I succeeded academically and in life; and my late uncle Charles Isiko and my aunt Monica Elizabeth Kagoya for giving me support and unconditional love when I needed it. Thanks to Uncle Charles Isabirye and his wife, Margaret for a lifelong training in life basics at my young and tender age while I was a student at Mwiri Primary School. I am grateful to my dear wife, Rose, and our children—Samuel, Samantha, Sherry, and Sheena Kaluya—for their love and understanding during the writing and preparation of this manuscript; even their disturbances were much appreciated, because they helped me to gather the courage to finish the book. I would also like to thank my brother Peter; my brother Fred and his wife, Patience; and Richard Waako for their love and for attending to my family while I was embarking on the many tasks of my busy schedule, among the writing of this book. I also dedicate this book and present copies to the schools I attended in Uganda and in the United States: Makerere High

School (A-level), Busoga College Mwiri (O-level), Namalemba Boarding Mixed and Mwiri Primary Schools (elementary schools), Dallas Baptist University, the University of Texas at Dallas, and Northcentral University.

Contents

Preface

For centuries, communities have been evolving and adjusting to the changes brought by time. This trend continues even today. However, have these communities been evolving for the better? Are communities like those in Africa being held back because of ignorance, backwardness, hopelessness, and poor leadership marred by corruption, paternalism, and selfishness? Do these African communities have the *audacity* to borrow a leaf from communities like those in Germany that evolved through the bringing down of the Berlin Wall? Or is the "Chinese way"—the mixing of Chinese culture and that of the West to enhance that country's current economic situation and develop it into a new and dynamic economic power, along with the gradual destruction of its own once cherished Communism to embrace a new Capitalist system—a lesson for Africans? Additionally, is Africa's backwardness causing it to be looked down upon by its Western and Asian trade partners? I presume this is so. Therefore, we must rise up audaciously to create an African continent that is able and credible enough to relate with the rest of the world while focusing on mutual interests—not a continent full of citizens who both evade facing their own realities and delude themselves into thinking that their existence is owed to them by those who destroyed what would be their incremental rise to modernity. We must also realize that we have remained in a state of backwardness, hopelessness, disease, etc., circumstances that have hindered our development for a long time.

Without underestimating the impact of the above, can we also affirm that the nature of statehood and the colonial national boundaries that define several African countries have been hindrances to the development and removal of total backwardness on the continent? Secondly, can we Africans continue to afford to sit back and wait for philanthropic organizations like the Bill and Melinda Gates Foundation and the Rockefeller Foundation, TV hosts and celebrities like Oprah Winfrey, and other donors, including the International Monetary Fund (IMF), the World Bank, and of course, the Western nations to part with their wealth and develop the continent? Do these philanthropists, foundations, organizations, and countries owe Africa a living? Furthermore, when will African leaders stop trotting around the Western world to attend conferences and summits that exclusively target aid for Africa and Africans? To what extent has this aid even been effective in the development of the African continent? All these questions are addressed in the discussions and insights in this book, and I encourage you, the reader, to have an unbiased mind-set when reading it—for it is not a mistake to take the step to read it. Ten percent of the sale of each book will be donated to New Horizon Christian Education Foundation, Inc., to help educate future leaders in Africa.

Thank you,

Professor M. D. Kaluya
Author

Acknowledgments

Acknowledgements go to iUniverse for reviewing the manuscript and publishing it as a finished product. I also thank the following people for their various contributions to the preparation of this manuscript: Professor Julius Sonko and his wife, Eva, for organization; Ms. Julie Niwankunda and Ms. Carolyne Eleanor for the reviews and additional research; Ms. Irene Kamami for editing the very first chapters; my cousin Susan Isiko Striba, PhD, for her counsel and direction on title selection; the professors at the University of Texas at Dallas, especially Professor Euel Elliott, for his insight, expertise, and direction; and the professors and administrators at Dallas Baptist University for receiving me and training me to be a useful servant of God. I am especially thankful to Ms. Rebecca Brown for her support in my earlier years as a new student from Africa. I am grateful to Hon. Prof. Philip Kaloki and his wife, Gloria, for their insight on African issues and their support in those first years in the United States. Special acknowledgements go to the Ugandan community in Dallas – Fort Worth Metroplex and other African communities in the same area; that I have interacted with for their support through thick and thin while making life work for us all in the Diaspora. My thanks also go to my colleagues and the students of Cedar Valley College and the Dallas County Community College District family (DCCCD) for all their contributions. Finally, thank you to my business associates at RMJ Business Solutions, LLC, in Hurst, Texas, and my pastor, John Musoke, and the entire congregation at Nations for Christ Church, Arlington, Texas, for the endless prayers over my life and the lives of my family members—God Bless you all!

Introduction

⌒⁀⌒

The Audacity to Change: Breaking the Berlin Wall in Africa is a critical piece that analyzes the ills of the African continent and exposes them to the entire world. The exposure is not meant to taint the continent but to provide an unbiased view of how to fully relate with it in terms of its growth and sustainable development. This is explained in ten chapters. The last chapter is the core; in it are solutions to the ills of the African continent. The word *backwardness* will appear a lot in this book. This is not an accident; it is used to sum up the ills the African continent and her people face every single day. The idea behind the book is based on the breaking of the Berlin Wall in Germany. The author does not wish to explain the forces that finally brought down the Berlin Wall, which allowed the eventual reintegration of East and West Germany to become a reality, but only to assert that these forces had engaged the wall for quite a long period of time before it finally fell. The fall of the Berlin Wall was the physical breakdown of the concrete wall, which permitted the two peoples to come together and enjoy the socioeconomic benefits that the integration brought forth.

In comparing the situation in Berlin to the African continent's level of backwardness, I see the majority of poor Africans facing similar circumstances daily, though the reality is that the wall of backwardness in Africa is not a physical barrier that warrants breaking, as happened in Germany. The term *backwardness* in this book encompasses the gruesome features that have proven to be impediments to Africa's success and consequently represent the wall that must be broken with determination. These features have kept the continent and her people in a state of poverty and hopelessness. *Backwardness*, as used in this book, can be attributed to a state of mind, one that is characteristic of a failure to reason and to question why, as Africans, we continue to live as though nothing is wrong with our surroundings. We continue to be surrounded by poverty, disease, ignorance, conflict, hate, endless wars, etc., but we seem to have no idea of how to address these issues. The failure or even the reluctance to gather solutions through research and critical thinking without the help of the Western countries leaves us in a state of backwardness. This backwardness, interestingly enough, is not limited to ordinary citizens; it is also an issue prevalent among the leaders of that great continent and among those of us who seem to represent the intellectual elite of Africa.

Chapter 1 introduces the reader to how societies have formed and are currently forming. This chapter also conveys the message to the reader that African society is yet to form but will if backwardness is eliminated. The failure of African reformation is grounded in how deeply rooted its backwardness has been; it is necessary to find the crucial elements that define this state of affairs today so that Africans can emerge as a society like the Germans did.

Chapter 2 is the beginning of the explanation as to why Africa has remained in a state of backwardness and what exactly constitutes *backwardness*. Chapter 3 continues this discussion by giving what the author calls "independent reviews by Africans" of the state of backwardness in which their continent exists. The contents in chapter 3 are not the works of the author but independent responses of individuals of African descent across the world, representing their views on Africa and her people. Chapter 4 presents the steps to the tedious process of removing backwardness from Africa. Chapter 5 is a call to embrace an ideology upon which the continent can build to come out of its backwardness. Chapter 6 describes and differentiates nations from states and the rights each enjoys as an entity. The purpose for this chapter is to provide the understanding that if Africa forged strategic relations with the rest of the world, the issue of backwardness would be a thing of the past because of the advantages that come with those relations. Chapter 7 is a call for Africans living outside the continent to act as the core in the development of the continent. Chapter 8 discourages the people of the African continent from depending on and consuming aid, because aid will never be effective in Africa, especially in the way it is currently being given and received. Chapter 9 calls for Africa to attain and embrace its own age of enlightenment just as other countries did theirs. Finally, chapter 10 lists and explains the solutions that must be undertaken for Africa to come out of its state of backwardness. I recommend this book to all readers as worthy of their time. For readers who are not Africans, like I am, the book will help them to determine strategic ways of relating to the continent of Africa. Those of us from Africa should embrace this book for its critical but necessary exposure to the rest of the world as the only way we shall come out of backwardness.

Professor M. D. Kaluya
Dallas, Texas, USA

Chapter One

~

The Evolution of Society

Society has developed through three overlapping stages—physical, vital, and mental ... physical realities, such as our survival, a life of fear and threat from without, and the need for complete deference to authority; ... vital needs and wants, including our desire to interact with others and expand and trade, come into their own; to the present emerging mental stage where understanding, knowledge, peace, freedom, democracy, the fulfillment and empowerment of the individual, the emergence of fast, complex organizations, and the extraordinary power of thought ... Beyond that is the spiritual stage of social evolution where mind is more fully developed to allow multi-sided awareness of truth, instead of the current limited capacity of mind, and where one connects with the spiritual Force that enables the ultimate flowering and transformation of life.

—Roy Posner

On November 9, 1989, a new society was formed in Europe. East and West Germany rejoined to form what we know today as Germany. To be more precise, the Berlin Wall fell on that day and paved way for the integration of the impoverished

5

East Germany with the wealthy West. As mentioned in the introduction, it is not my goal to explain the forces that finally brought down the wall and allowed the integration to become a reality; I want to point out, however, that these forces had been acting against the wall for a considerable time before finally breaking it down. The fall of the Berlin Wall refers to the physical destruction of the concrete wall, which allowed the poor East Germans access to the much-needed socioeconomic benefits of reintegration. I compare the Berlin wall to the African continent's level of backwardness. I do not use the word *backwardness* in a derogatory manner but as term to encompass what has been the cause of Africa's woes for quite a long time. The backwardness I am addressing is the unwanted and deplorable circumstances the majority of poor Africans face every single day. In reality, African backwardness is not the result of any physical barriers or walls that can be broken like the one in Germany. Backwardness in this book refers to those features that have proved to be impediments to Africa's success and consequently represent an imaginary wall that can only be destroyed by determination. These features have kept the continent and its people in a state of poverty and hopelessness. Physical walls, according to Daniel Shorr,[1] exist elsewhere, "the one between the Israelis and the Palestinians for example." He also added that "a wall can mean not only closed borders but closed minds. In Iran today, strict suppression of dissent is met by the technology of freedom: the internet, which breaks down walls."

I attribute backwardness to a state of mind, one that is characterized by the failure to reason and to question the way in which we as Africans are living. We continue to live with poverty, disease, ignorance, unnecessary conflict, hate, and wars. Most of us seem to care little about how we can address these issues. Our failure or even reluctance to gather solutions and exercise consciousness through critical thinking without the help of the Western world leaves us in a state of backwardness. This backwardness, however, is prevalent not only among ordinary citizens, but also among the leaders and the intellectuals of the continent.

What this chapter covers is the general discussion of how deep our backwardness has been and which crucial elements define this state of affairs today and hinder the emergence of a society similar to what evolved out of East and West Germany.

Despite the modern times in which we live, Africa still experiences backwardness, ignorance, disease, and conflict (both political and ethnic). In this chapter, I introduce you to the process societies go through before they become modern. I believe it's important to know where societies came from, because they did not start out in their modern form. The ever-increasing search for knowledge by scientists has revealed to us that the earth is estimated to have been created 4.6 billion years ago. And the first human-like animals started emerging about fourteen million years ago. These humans were called *hominids*, i.e., animals that were like human beings. Evolutionary scientists have proved that we all came from early primates and went on evolving until we started walking on two legs. Initially, we were all *quadri-pedal*, or four-legged, like chimpanzees, and then we developed the skill of walking on two legs.

About 1.8 to 1.3 million years ago, a certain creature known as *Homo erectus* evolved. These creatures, as illustrated in figure 1, could walk upright, as the word *erectus* suggests. They began using fire just as the history books tell us. The discovery of fire was very important because they could use it to cook and roast food and keep warm. These were just groups of human-like animals, who were not living in highly organized societies. They did not have any hierarchical administration whatsoever. It was not until ten-plus thousand years ago that civilizations like that of Babylon and Mesopotamia arose. They started to deal in crops and animals as far back as 7,002 years ago, when the human being started living a civilized life. What does living a civilized life mean? It means the once uncivilized start living by cooperation amongst themselves rather than conflicting and competing with one another. This is the element of civilization. Learning how to divide jobs is an aspect of civilization—we can ration jobs, "You do this, and I or they do that." This is the actual part of civilization I am trying to address here.

Figure 1: *Homo erectus* being as he might have looked

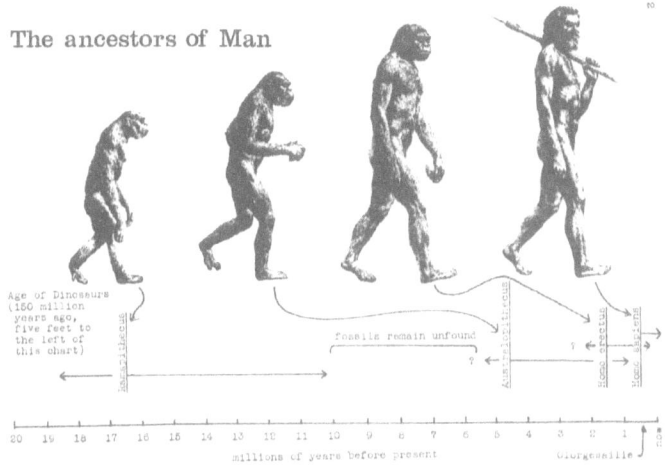

Figure 2: This figure shows the progression of human beings through evolutionary stages.

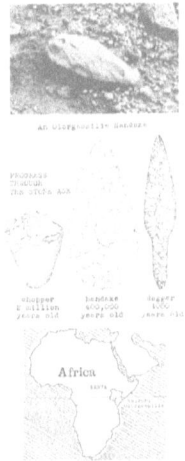

Figure 3: Some of the tools developed by the first human beings through their creativity and civilization are displayed in this picture. The Olorgesailie is found one hundred miles south of the equator on the floor of Kenya's Rift Valley, where the earth's crust cracked open millions of years ago. The three pictures are credited to Mr. Rensberger, the Alicia Patterson Foundation, and the L. S. B. Leakey Foundation.

In social evolution and organization, we have what I call a primer, illustrated in figure 4. The primer acts as the change in science and technology. When science and technology in a society change, society will change either for better or worse; this depends on where the two variables are heading. If the variables χ and γ are heading downward, meaning nobody is caring or thinking forward, the worst outcome will prevail, but if they are trending upward through discoveries and inventions, the better part of science and technology will be achieved. So scientific and technological development for the better is a primer to changing the way society does things.

When fire was discovered by the human beings, as already mentioned, there were a lot of changes. Before the use of fire was understood, the human-like beings of the time were living under trees and were called tree dwellers because they could not go into the caves where they could not see. Fire created an opportunity for the humans of the time to go into the caves with light. They used fire to expel the darkness and warm the interior of the once very damp caves, thereby chasing snakes and other dangerous animals that could harm them from the caves. They then stopped dwelling under the trees and became cave dwellers. Consequently, the discovery of fire to them was the primer to change in their society at that time.

In addition to being the primer of the change of dwelling place, fire also changed the way they ate. These human-like beings started eating roasted instead of raw meat. The eating of cooked food perhaps changed both the digestive systems and physiological makeup of the humans. Additionally, they no longer had the task of gnawing and thus did not need to have such strong jaws. Because they were eating softer food, they could develop a finer shape to their jaws. What is more interesting is that all these changes came about as a result of the discovery of fire.

Today, we celebrate another crucial development in the world described by Thomas Friedman[2] in his national bestseller, *The Lexus and the Olive Tree*, which is the democratization of technology facilitated by the invention of the Internet. Friedman argues that democratization of technology emanates from several innovations that came of age in the 1980s, including computerization, telecommunications, miniaturization, compression technology, and digitization. What Friedman is telling us is that simply embracing the use of technology across the globe with little or no constraints on the consumer is the primer to the widespread sharing of information; as a result, countries and their people can come together through the power of the Internet. Despite the fact that many countries are now connected on the global Internet grid, African countries still struggle to attain such a reality. Yet the simple truth of our time is that national boundaries have become a thing of the past, because the world has become interconnected into one global village. Recently, the East African countries started on a journey of connecting the member states to high-speed Internet using broadband cables. This is a good step for the leaders in those countries to take. Let corruption, tribal conflicts, and poor planning be the ways of the past, because if they stop us from embracing the new global village, our backwardness will continue to limit the progress of our nations.

Illustration of a primer:

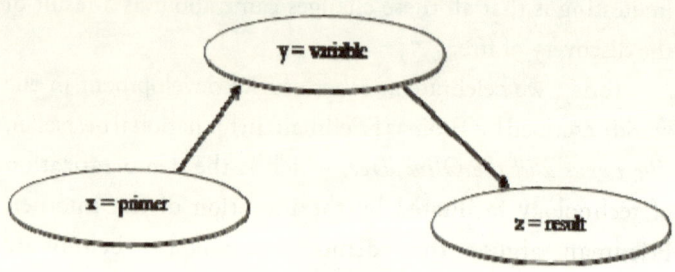

Figure: 4
*The primer X must be present to influence the
variable Y to produce the result Z.*

African leaders in general must undertake the task of understanding society more deeply before they can engage the problems within their own as they strive to utilize a specific primer to redeem their people out of poverty, disease, and backwardness. The most important question African leaders need to ask of themselves is: where did society come from? As leaders, they must know the answer to this question. The breaking of the Berlin Wall seems to be the most recent event illustrating how societies emerge in these modern times. It should be a lesson to African leaders. Consequently, African leaders must mobilize their people to break the wall of backwardness just as the Germans broke the Berlin Wall. In doing so, African leaders would be setting mobilization of the masses into motion for the cause: breaking the wall of backwardness. The idea of mobilization of the masses must be consciously carried out based on certain principles that will create communities that are capable of sustaining themselves both in the internal and external environments.

The people of Africa must be close to their leaders in order to support them for the cause of development. African leaders have been fond of meandering about—flying from continent to continent, especially to the Western capitals to attend aid conferences. Yet they know the problems facing Africa and how these problems can best be solved even when aid is effectively used. The idea of aid effectiveness will be addressed in a later chapter. Many people can advance the argument that we Africans lack science, but this is not true. Our friends in the Asian world have developed only in the last forty-five years. For instance, in the 1960s, South Korea was not very different from many of our African states; it was at about the same level of development as most of the African nations were at the time, as were some other countries like Thailand and Malaysia. Perhaps we should mention that one of the best qualities of a right-thinking individual, according to one philosopher, are "being a thinker, having some social stature or being sociable in the community, and lastly bearing leadership qualities."[3] To break the wall of backwardness, we must embrace the words of this philosopher.

You can find more on this topic in an encyclopedia if you want to expand your knowledge, but let me take you to a quotation from Simon Nkanda's[4] book, *The Monarch's Dream: Chief Manana's Wake-Up Call to Africa*. The following is one of Izumba's speech's highlights (Izumba is the character portrayed by the author as a foreign-educated citizen who heads back home to Africa after college). This is what he said:

> Ladies and Gentlemen, the time is now that our culture begins to take a different course aimed at a future society filled with creative thinkers. A society of

people who spent time thinking of ways … to improve our quality of life in the same way our ancestors learned to tackle life by making tools for hunting, tilling the land, building shelters, clothing material, ornaments, and many other things that we know still exist to this day. We must prepare our youth to face this challenge and become enculturated to the ideal of original thinking.[5]

This quotation is profound and brings out the message I am trying to put across to you, the reader. We Africans have all the necessary tools to reason and invent. Using those skills, our ancestors developed society to the current level. The rate at which we have embraced civilization in Africa has been very slow, yet real civilization started long ago when human beings started living in organized societies. It's noted that our ancestors were human beings, all right, but they were not yet civilized. They were hunting in small groups, each one looking for survival. Let me ask again: what does civilization mean? So many answers can be given to this question, but what if we say that civilization is the development of the cooperative instinct? When one group is able to cooperate with another group in a regulated manner, the resulting effect is civilization. According to scientists who study the brain, the human brain has two parts; one of them is called the *hypothalamus* and it controls instincts like breathing and blinking. These actions are not controlled consciously; they just simply happen. The second part of the brain, called the *encephalon*, is the part that is conscious of what you can do or cannot do. The activities controlled by the conscious parts of the brain are the ones that build up civilization. It is more scientific to make the argument that regardless of the concentration of the *encephalon*, all communities on Planet Earth, including those in Africa, must be advanced in civilization today. Failure to speed up the rate at which Africa is civilizing will leave us in a state of backwardness.

Chapter Two

What Has Caused Africa to Remain in a State of Backwardness?

Part I

*Humans are woefully unaware of gaps
in their own self-knowledge.*
—Caputo and Dunning[6]

We can only describe our backwardness by thinking in terms of the advancements that have ranged from superstitious, ethnocentric thinking to philosophy. In fact, we can divide the knowledge of the last two millennia or more into two categories: organic and mechanical. During the time of Socrates, about two thousand years ago, the rationalist line of thinking emerged and started challenging the metaphysical way of looking at the world. These two tendencies were later called mechanic and organic, that's to say, rational and metaphysical.

The metaphysical deals with supernatural powers, the idea that you do not have to worry because God will take care of you (i.e., all that has befallen you, for instance, poverty or richness, is God's doing). This is the idea of metaphysics. The notion that people will get whatever God wanted them to get is fundamental in the African context and surely contributes to the stagnation in backwardness that is prevalent across the continent. However, rationalism has started making inroads in Africa; people who think about what God has for them but only to a certain degree are now emerging. The saying that "God helps those who help themselves" is taking center stage in some African societies. What I am trying to bring to your attention is that Africans have picked up the kind of thinking necessary to come out of backwardness but have done so in a sluggish manner. This means that our people are advancing from superstition to philosophy (i.e., from metaphysics to rationality).

The rationality philosophy proposes a cause-and-effect reality. We all know that in life, there is a reason why things happen. Of course, they do not just happen from above, as some people may want us to believe; a lot of what happens is based on what we do here, in other words, cause and effect. For instance, some people are poor because they are lazy, or they are poor because the economic conditions in their country are inequitable. Additionally, Western countries and the Asian tigers, with China at the forefront, are polluting the ozone layer with gas emissions from factories and fuel-guzzling vehicles. This pollution is not coming from above; it's human made. We should focus our attention broadly while looking at the world. Before Socrates' influence on many philosophers, we had people called the Sophists; they were viewed as legalists and were specialists in rhetoric and persuasion. The Sophists used these means to persuade people to join their side. But then Socrates came and started questioning things (i.e., the how and why questions started taking shape) perhaps to demand facts and understanding. Africa will continue to be backward if we fail to question why things are happening the way they are. We need to develop at a very fast rate the idea of being thinkers and creators. We need to become independent thinkers. Once we master this, backwardness will be history and behind our backs.

The other problem that is very crucial is that of ideology. Ideology is a very big problem for Africa, and we shall not go far if it's not solved. For instance, people in the management field end up causing organizations to collapse, because they have not looked at what they are doing from a historical perspective. In managing society, we must not use guesswork. It's said that man is a habitual creature. He seeks pleasure and avoids pain. The human being is not programmed just as God wants, but he (the human being) also wants to have a good life. The problem is that human beings cannot have good lives all the time; there must be a time for sacrifice. Economists, argue that human beings exhibit behaviors that are mostly focused at maximizing utility in what they do. The economists also argue that since utility maximization depends on the availability of resources, communities or individuals without these resources will in most cases fail to maximize their intended levels of utility. Moreover, resource exploitation requires skills; without these skills, the communities will lag behind regardless of the amount of unexploited resources they might have. Most African countries are rich in resources in the ground; however, the lack of skills and the ideology to impart knowledge and consciousness to the citizens to exploit what is in their environment will make Africa suffer for years. Today, these factors prevent Africa as a continent from fully maximizing the utility of its abundant resources. The saying that "knowledge is based on experience" is also important in a manager's role. If you have not experienced something, you cannot know what it is all about. Therefore, the issue of ideology and political morality stand to be the biggest problems facing the African continent and ultimately a cause of its backwardness. We lack focus in our way forward in almost everything, and as a result, we are exploited greatly by other countries that developed before us. We should stop blaming others for our own follies and stop always expecting someone to come rescue us from our predicaments. What happened in the past, namely colonialism, we must leave the past and forge a way forward.

The human race across the globe has gone through a lot, and on a continent like Africa, people have tended to believe in what came before them, which has curtailed a great part of its people's thinking capacities.

Furthermore, the idea that African leaders face ideological bankruptcy in getting their people out of this thinking rut is very real and needs attention by those very people involved. Our leaders have tended to look at things that do not matter and forget those that do matter. After colonialism or immediately after a country gains independence, its problem is not deciding who should take what position but establishing a state that can look into the problems of the population. Problems in Zimbabwe today are a real example of what I am talking about here. The problem in Zimbabwe today is a failure to establish state leadership—leadership that is crucial and effective in addressing the affairs of the people of that country. In other words, the state as an entity is the main problem in this scenario, not who should assume which position in the state. Speaking of Zimbabwe, most African nations are on the brink of collapse for lack of statehood, whose function is to emancipate and create a people who are creative, knowledgeable, nationalistic, and hopeful to change the nation for better and not for worse.

Furthermore, the people make up the state, and they have a responsibility to determine who assumes which position to help them solve their endless problems. But a lack of determination by the people to make the decisions and choose the right leaders is what has made Africa lag behind. We simply have no way of determining how to govern ourselves—the infighting across borders and within ethnic groups in many African nations resonates around this backwardness. Yet, if we determined a way of choosing our leaders, then democracy would take root in our societies. It is true that political leaders across the world have faced problems in which religious ideologies have come into play, and some leaders have chosen to lead their countries on such ideologies. We should be aware that the Catholics, Protestants, and Muslims have brought in religious ideologies that today are very influential in our societies. Nonetheless, should we use any of these ideologies to represent society? Absolutely not! What we need to do is to strike a balance amongst all these societal ideologies. If we allow religious ideologies to influence the political agenda, then we are simply embracing backwardness.

Societies have different problems that need, not a particular religious ideology to solve them, but well-balanced political solutions entrenched within the state institutions. In many parts of rural Africa, farmers need to develop their fields and market their products, and the best way to satisfy these farmers is for leaders to meet their demands through access to better roads, farming incentives like credit schemes, markets for their produce, and most important, adequate educational facilities to increase the effectiveness of the nation's human resources. Our religious ideologies will not solve what I have just described in this chapter, and they have not done so in the past. On the other hand, knowing that there are vested interest groups in society, the way forward must be to modernize ourselves in form and thinking. These modernization programs must be mass-oriented and not for marginal benefits. It should be noted that mass-orienting our modernization programs, together with the accommodation of all other societal interests, should be part and parcel of any political ideology.

In fact, achieving a truly modernized society will only require one thing, getting people out of backwardness, and that is an "ideology" and nothing else. In doing so, a determination to achieve common ideas must be sought. One proponent of American democracy, Alexis de Tocqueville,[7] in his book, *Democracy in America*, suggested that a "nation without common ideas has no common action, and without common action, men still exist, but a social body does not." It's up to the political leaders in Africa to build support along a political ideology or common ideas that represent the masses, which should be modern-centric to match the times of the day. Such an ideology should be modern-centric because if you do not modernize, you perish. Communities like those of the American Indians of North America and the Incas and Aztecs of South America have all perished or are on the verge of perishing because they did not modernize their societies.

Chapter Three

✿

What Has Caused Africa to Remain in a State of Backwardness?

Part II
(A View of Africans by Africans)

They have backward innocence—[I] do not know what they don't have or what they can't do. 2. They are friendly and warm ... [A] people of that nature are puzzling!
—Lieutenant Sabiti Kabuchu, Kampala, Uganda

This chapter is what I call a "bonus" chapter, because it emphasizes our state of backwardness. In order to make this emphasis, I turned to some common views that cause us Africans to remain fully in a state of what I can call "freely being backward." These views were exclusively collected by one journalist, Mr. Timothy Kalyegira[8] in response to an online question to a group of people from Africa. From May 14, 2006, to April 2, 2009, Mr. Timothy Kalyegira collected views from over one hundred African citizens who have lived in, visited, transited through, or traveled in at least two African countries. The answers are in response to the question below, but they fully explain our continued state of backwardness.

The question was: **"From your traveling around Africa, what is the thing about Africans that puzzles you the most?"**

The following are some of the over one hundred responses. These are not my responses but those given to Mr. Kalyegira from a number of people whose names and places of residence I have listed after their response.

"Our inability to plan, especially long-term." —**Daniel Kalinaki, Kampala, Uganda**

"I'm puzzled by the religious adoration of anybody in authority." —**James Onen, Kampala, Uganda**

"Our complacent attitude towards poverty. People are very poor but there is a general acceptance that the rulers are the ones who have a right to money and a good quality of life (health, education, housing) while the rest happily go about with their hard lives (our fate!). They don't think they deserve better." —**Jackie Nyagahima, Entebbe, Uganda**

"Tough question. I would cite the maverick ideology, [that is] fly by the seat of the pants or makeshift attitude. A certain lack of passion and planning." —**Tom Ogwang, Gulu, Uganda**

"What puzzles me is Africans' lack of regard for time." —**Sonia Kiconco Rees, Kampala, Uganda**

"People expecting to earn without working: [taking of] commission; begging; complacency with subsistence living;

relying too much on nature." —**Henry Manyire, Kampala, Uganda**

"Endless greed. Everywhere you go in Africa, it's that. You set up a task force to investigate corruption and on that task force is a chairman who [himself] should be investigated for corruption. It's crazy!" —**Jaffer Remo, Kampala, Uganda**

"The lack of shame. And I mean shame in a philosophical way." —**Charles Onyango-Obbo, Nairobi, Kenya**

"The thing that puzzles me is their backwardness. When will they ever develop?" —**Vianey Kabera, Kigali, Rwanda**

"Lack of appreciation for the next generation and legacy." —**Arthur Ntengwe, Kampala, Uganda**

"The fact that they ran towards a violent scene rather than away from it." —**Trupti Shah, Nairobi, Kenya**

"The way we try to copy White people and then turn around and blame them for things that are our fault. Then how we always seem to discourage enterprise." —**Dennis Matanda, Kampala, Uganda**

"1. They have backward innocence—[I] do not know what they don't have or what they can't do. 2. They are friendly and warm … [A] people of that nature are puzzling!" —**Lieutenant Sabiti Kabuchu, Kampala, Uganda**

"It is [the] laissez faire attitude." —**Stephen Asiimwe, Kampala, Uganda**

"The faith, the positive attitude with which they take some hard knocks that are always coming at them." —**Loy Nabeta, Dar es Salaam, Tanzania**

"What puzzles me the most about Africans is how they want to go somewhere, get up in the morning, dress up, hit the road, leaving the map and compass boxed at home. How will they get there? Try the genius!" —**Susan Nangwale, Kampala, Uganda**

"I must say it is our dismal time-keeping." —**Valentine Rwegasira, London, United Kingdom**

"They seem unbothered by the shabbiness of their surroundings." —**Francis Onapito Ekomoloit, Kampala, Uganda**

"Very joyous [in spite of] the daily quagmires we face. Is it masochism? Also, we hate reading! If only Africans could read more." —**Winston ("TShaka") Mayanja, Kampala, Uganda**

"Our inability to risk our material objects to defend our principles." —**Andrew Mwenda, Kampala, Uganda**

"About my view [what] puzzled me in Africa is, people are more relying on others [rather] than fighting for themselves in order to get out of from where they are. 2. Compare[d] to where I'm now, meaning Europe, the people in Africa look happier with all the complicated problems they are in." —**Shewaye Legesse, Berlin, Germany**

"The remarkable inability, amid all the suffering, to see that they should hold their governments accountable for improving their lives." —**Conrad Nkutu, Kampala, Uganda**

"What shocks me [for example] is how the majority of Congolese [are] resigned to their fate. Wake [up], dress nicely, and party all night from Monday to Monday." —**Frank Nyakairu, Kampala, Uganda**

"Disturbs more like. Lack of ambition." —**Paul Busharizi, Kampala, Uganda**

"Their ignorance. 99 percent of them are ignorant about everything. They are ignorant even about themselves." —**Jolly Kanimba, Kampala, Uganda**

"Africans are simple, superstitious, uncreative and wealth exploiters." —**Allan Sekamatte, Kampala, Uganda**

"Failure to take detail seriously." —**Paul Nyangabyaki, Kampala, Uganda**

"We are not bothered, so we do not pay attention to detail and for the same reason we accept (almost) anything from anyone." —**Rhona Baingana, Kampala, Uganda**

"The complacency; the fact that people seem to accept things as they are. Even those who seem to have prescriptions for the issues." —**Juliet Nabwire, Kampala, Uganda**

"We are crazy. First of all, we are a puzzle in ourselves: we are foreigners here in our own lands and [yet] we are [also] foreigners when we are in Europe and America. We are crazy!" —**Susan Kakuhikire, Kampala, Uganda**

"[The] insatiable greed for everything." —**Arthur Ruberantwari, Entebbe, Uganda**

"What puzzled me most is that people in all three countries [I visited] were comfortable throwing litter all over their environs." —**Charity Ahimbisibwe, Kampala, Uganda**

"I am always amazed at Africans' ability to rise above their problems by making light of them." —**Nassozi Muwanga, Kampala, Uganda**

"They are many but failure to appreciate contemporary statehood takes the meat." —**Asuman Bisiika, Kampala, Uganda**

"Complacency and complaining." —**Emily Gakiza, Kampala, Uganda**

"Self-destructive tendencies. An inherent frustration, a tendency to spoil, to despise one's own … a general neglect of resources, of assets." —**Michael Bakibinga, Kampala, Uganda**

"Without any hesitation, lack of initiative, a resignation to fate and inability to comprehend that one can determine one's destiny, hence we wait for our 'leaders' to guide and advise us. This ranges from the Muslim in Gambia to the South African and our next-door neighbors in Rwanda. Africans trust and lean on their leaders too much and our problems will always invariably be linked to poor leadership." —**Pamela Tibihikira Kalyegira, Kampala, Uganda**

"Lack of respect for formal rules." —**Peter Mwesige, Kampala, Uganda**

"Absence of shame; they don't blush whatever the circumstances." —**Andrew Kasirye, Kampala, Uganda**

"Their love for partying." —**Julius Dingisha, Kampala, Uganda**

"Our happy-go-lucky nature, in spite of our myriad problems. However, our deep-rooted jealousies counter that." —**Raymond Byabazaire, Kampala, Uganda**

"It's that air of perpetually waiting for humanitarian intervention. A beggar mentality across [the] board, whether [it is the] elite or peasants." —**Robert Shaka, Kampala, Uganda**

"Their inability to save. They believe in spending for the moment." —**Arthur Kitakufe, Kampala, Uganda**

"Corruption." —**Banteyehun Haile, Kampala, Uganda**

"I have come across hundreds of brilliant minds who are leaders in their own right, with natural resources probably worth trillions of dollars. What else can be done to unlock greatness in our continent? That's what puzzles me." —**Ethan Mussolini, Kampala, Uganda**

"The majority's belief [in] or recourse to the supernatural, [other] worldly, or divine when confronted by a problem. This tendency transcends all strata of society regardless of their [nurturing.]" —**Lieutenant-Colonel Matthew Gureme, Kampala, Uganda**

"Strong, optimistic, diverse, and [unyielding] even in [the] worst of circumstances." —**William Babigumira, Kampala, Uganda**

"Lack of a sense of when they err." —**Joachim Buwembo, Kampala, Uganda**

"Most Africans I met were trying to fit either in their own countries or abroad. They are trying to find [a] social ethic that [defines] them and their world and they are confused but inexplicably optimistic about the future." —**Angelo Izama, Kampala, Uganda**

"Patience in the face of incompetence and inertia." —**Ian Ibara, Kampala, Uganda**

"Our [tendency] to procrastinate … Less do it yourself and always seeking external factors to sort our destiny. We just don't know how to own up." —**Andrew Lubega, Kampala, Uganda**

"Easily manipulated. Don't stand up to bullies." —**James Masaba, Kampala, Uganda**

"The fear of intellectual daring. Our people prefer pretensions to thought, [to] thought proper. It is funny how [in Africa] intelligence is not [what] intelligence does but as it postures." —**Philip Matogo, Luwero, Uganda**

"Lack of ingenuity. Lack of organization of people unless there is [direct personal benefit.]" —**Winfred Rukidi, Kampala, Uganda**

"The all-too-common refusal to connect the events and actions that directly affect their lives, unless these events are expressions of violence." —**Alan Tacca, Jinja, Uganda**

"Africans are liars, selfish, very disorganized, and yes some are very dirty … I am surprised how Africans can survive under such [a] horrible lifestyle year after year." —**Shawn Ray Makumbi, Kampala, Uganda**

"The thing that puzzles me the most about Africans is their ineptitude in their daily work." —**Anthony Ruberantwari, Entebbe, Uganda**

"Their aversion to keeping the law." —**Ben Mwine, Kampala, Uganda**

"The casual way we tend to deal with serious matters. We lack attention to detail [in the way we approach] life and we want to have free things all the time irrespective of the cost. We are highly sociable people, but we lack discipline, ethics, and integrity especially when it comes to power and money. Even PhD holders become uncultured and can't react differently. Lack of genuine remorse when we do wrong also puzzles me lots and it is common here in Africa." —**Lameck Kiirya, Fort Portal, Uganda**

"Lack of inspiration in the sense of ideas and creativity." —**Tony Otoa Jr., London, United Kingdom**

"[How we are] little bothered about time." —**Achilles Kiwanuka, Kampala, Uganda**

"Why we still think Whites are much better than us. We hero worship them and elevate them to superhuman status. [Lack] of self-esteem and self-worth. We don't have much faith in our abilities [and] talents. It's a new form of slavery—of the mind!" —**Sheila Kulubya, Kampala, Uganda**

"Disorder in her cities yet people seem [to be] intelligent!" —**Michael Wangusa, Kampala, Uganda**

"Some kind of amazing laziness which beats me sometimes. Zambians take the cup [in this]. Showing off and extravagance is another character very typical of Africans; that's why we shall never develop." —**Barbara Bamanya, Lusaka, Zambia**

"The fear of facing the truth, especially if not favorable." —**Grace Mayanja, Kampala, Uganda**

"A happy people in spite of our economic hardships." —**Edward Magumba, Jinja, Uganda**

"[How] the White man lives a better life [in the African countries I have visited than the native Africans] [and how] the Black man is doing his best to please the White man." —**Didas Bakunzi, Kampala, Uganda**

"The thing that puzzles most is our total lack of shame. We glorify corruption and plunder and the honest morals are disregarded." —**Obed Kamugisha, Kampala, Uganda**

"Africans … keep quiet about the things that really matter." —**Kathy Kateera, Kampala, Uganda**

"Laziness. They have no urge to work which [leads] to our being dependent, corrupt, thugs, [and] wanting free things." —**Charles Mugisha, Kampala, Uganda**

"The propensity [for] the easy life without hard work." —**Peter Byarugaba, Kampala, Uganda**

"What puzzles me to no end about [us] Africans is the difficulty we have in grasping deep philosophical and abstract thought and the broadest and most far-ranging ideas, the difficulty in concentrating mentally and how difficult we find it to master minute craftsmanship and detail, all of which are the basis for creating advanced civilizations. Even when motivated by the best of intentions, our efforts almost always flounder in the face of this debilitating limitation—the hard time we have in getting our minds to concentrate. Decades of elite education, international travel, and residency in the sophisticated Western countries, and an affluent middle-class standard of living, seem to have done little to overcome this limitation." —**Timothy Kalyegira, Kampala, Uganda**

"What drives me insane is that in most cases they do not act in their own interests." —**Lieutenant-Colonel Moses Rwakitarate, Kampala, Uganda**

"They forget many times that they have to stand in a [queue]. They are eager to jump the queue but can't sometimes. [At international airports] many want to be seen [as being] frequent fliers." —**Barbara Bitangaro, Kampala, Uganda**

"Just as [I] believe in White mental and Black physical superiority, I get puzzled [over] why we can't learn from the experiences of those ahead of us. I guess it proves the above." —**Samson Bill Nyatia, Kampala, Uganda**

"The belief that they are just part of the system put [up] by someone else and they cannot change it." —**Ben Wandera, Kampala, Uganda**

"What puzzles me is the contradiction: people are intelligent and resourceful but feel and act inferior, while being defiant and patriotic at the same time." —**Mark Ssali, Kampala, Uganda**

"In one word: laissez faire attitude to life, [that is] as long as I eat and sleep, then nothing beyond that matters." —**Paul Nsibuka, Kampala, Uganda**

"Untidiness and lack of regard for fellow Africans." —**Cornelius Gulere, Kampala, Uganda**

"In the countries I have traveled in Africa, what beats my understanding is [that] public toilets are either dirty or completely run-down, whether in Uganda, Kenya, Tanzania, Rwanda, Burundi, the Democratic Republic of Congo, [or] Congo Brazzaville, yet we get surprised when things from [the] national level to [the] personal level get run-down." —**Alec Muhoho, Kampala, Uganda**

"What puzzles me is why people are fascinated by Idi Amin." —**Tony Ofungi, Kampala, Uganda**

"Superstitions, poor time-keeping, disorganization, poverty, and strong family bonds." —**Patrick Kamara, Kampala, Uganda**

"The lack of a sense of public and civic responsibility. Privately, [our public officials] live a comfortable, decent life, but they can't seem to apply these same standards in their homes to their public offices." —**Bernard Tabaire, Kampala, Uganda**

"How we settle for much less. How we feel that people from more developed countries are better than us in all aspects (including morals). The fact that we are survivors. We are and tend to be quite a happy lot." —**Julie Nayiga, Kampala, Uganda**

"That's been a puzzling question. I guess there are loads of [contradictions like] respect then disrespect, love of life then recklessness, move to town then happy in a slum. Where is this race going?" —**Margaret Wandera, Kampala, Uganda**

"It's the lack of self-confidence. Beyond the exterior is a deep-rooted low self-esteem that manifests [itself] in a variety of ways. Two ways I see: fear and emphasis on tangible rather than intangible resources." —**Martin Barungi, Kampala, Uganda**

"That we refuse to outgrow our peasant mentality. That we remain chronically and lethargic [ally] … indifferent to the important things in life." —**Alan Kasujja, Kampala, Uganda**

"Wanting to be involved in each other's lives … Africans feel they have a responsibility towards and a relationship with everyone. [The reason] why a taxi guy will call you uncle and me sister. The reason your [social events] like weddings are like clan and village reunions. The reason for nepotism … That collectiveness is what I mean." —**Helen Nyana, Kampala, Uganda**

"Lack of ambition. Your average African is quite content with his hut, which he calls his mansion, his three or four wives, and his horde of malnourished children running around naked. Even a 'rich' African doesn't see beyond his money, flashy cars, and big house." —**Fideri Kirungi, New York, USA**

"One thing I have seen in all our countries and which is common to the human race is that we do not learn from history. This aspect is more expressed in Africans than anywhere else." —**Henry Bagazonzya, Washington DC, USA**

"That [the leaders] all do not care about changing the lives of the poor, and they seem satisfied playing in the mud in which they are stuck, in terms of development." —**Wafula Oguttu, Kampala, Uganda**

"What puzzles me most is Africans' failure to recognize their 'Underdeveloped continent despite having resources. Facilities appear run-down save for South Africa.'" —**Henry Ssali, Kampala, Uganda**

"That a continent with so much potential and people who seem so much smarter than [other people in] so many places … seems so dire. Are we opportunists? Lazy? Or just buying time? Why do we have a 'me and my stomach' mentality and not a 'For God and my country and countrymen' one?" —**Jackie Bageire, Texas, USA**

"My answer is not about me but about [White] friends … who travel around Africa. What puzzles them is that the moment they meet any African, of whatever status (whether minister or beggar), the African automatically assumes that they (the Whites) are rich and tries to get the Whites to solve their financial problems … My friends say that this happens in all the countries they visit in Africa." —**Soogi Katende, Kampala, Uganda**

"It is that laissez faire attitude." —**Sam Obbo, Kampala, Uganda**

"What's puzzling about Africans is their lack of perseverance in what they want to do, craze for easy life and free things, adoration of Whites, and failure to work together." —**Norbert Mukasa, Kampala, Uganda**

"The thing that puzzles me most is the naivety of people and the similarity of the lifestyle amongst the common people. And everywhere you go, the African elite pretend a lot and are corrupted very much. They tend to maximize their own benefit. Sometimes you can't blame the [Whites] for doing the things they are doing to Africa because the people never wake up and those who are suppose[d] to understand what is going on … take advantage of the situation. So if you are never going to realize you are being cheated, they might as well rob you. That's what puzzles me from the little I've seen and read."
—Nigist Tilahun, Addis Ababa, Ethiopia

"I feel puzzled and angry that Africans are not able to pool their resources to their advantage. We seem to rely so much on foreigners to help us convert our resources into wealth. Look everywhere: if it is not the Europeans, it is the Indians or Lebanese at the centre of all enterprise. Africans are just employees earning a pittance. Maybe it is our leaders. Because look at Dubai; it is a monarchy but … that Emirate is ahead. Yet oil ranks number four on its list of [foreign exchange] earners." **—Moses Serugo, Kampala, Uganda**

"For me the thing that puzzles me the most is the amazing level of natural resource endowment sitting side by side with the most nail-biting poverty. I am also puzzled by how many Africans cannot seem to see (or have they chosen to ignore) the obvious in how to get things done. Equally puzzling but no longer surprising is how politicians replicate problems from other countries in their own as if they have just come from another planet!" **—John Bigyemano, Kampala, Uganda**

"I am puzzled by poor people's desire to cling onto life despite circumstances that would have dictated that they throw in the towel." —**James Mukanga, Kampala, Uganda**

"Africans like throwing rubbish through car and bus windows. The sheer fact of almost all African cities having sprawling slums home to half their population!" —**Martin Geria, Kampala, Uganda**

"That we are so stoical. In a Mozambique hospital, four mothers sat quietly by a bed shared by their four children. Their silence seemed so wrong!" —**Lilliane Barenzi, Kampala, Uganda**

"Africans are inherently timid. Few believe in their own abilities." —**Eric Naigambi, Kampala, Uganda**

"The fact that blacks treat fellow blacks less than the Whites, i.e., you will take 20 minutes more at immigration than the Whites, regardless of whether you are traveling with a White guy. It's everywhere, from the airline hostess, hotels, and shops. Crazy world!" —**Joseph Kwemala, Monrovia, Liberia**

"The thing that puzzles me the most is how Africans think the world (their particular countries) owes them a living simply because they were born there. We get easily comfortable with what we have around us and never strive to achieve more. Bottom line: we hate hassle even if it means reaping in the end. Rather than climb up a mango tree and pick a mango, we would sit under the tree and wait for it to fall down. I wouldn't really call that lazy. It's more of being carefree."
—**John Kimbe, Kampala, Uganda**

"What puzzles me is why we Africans try so hard to emulate our colonial masters yet our masters mistreated us. Maybe that's why we mistreat each other so much." —**Juliet Nsiima, Kigali, Rwanda**

"The usual: the laidback attitude … all over the continent. Oh dear! Oh dear." —**Franco Baitwa, Kampala, Uganda**

"Most Africans are not sincere. [They] try to cheat you when [they] realize you are a visitor. Most Africans [are] disorganized in everything!" —**Robert Mugagga, Kampala, Uganda**

"The indifference of our rulers. They do not care. Even the enlightened and so much celebrated have lost direction. I'm turning 45 next February [2007]. All this time I've been around, nothing has changed about Africa. It is the same story. Poverty! I have resigned. I have lost hope." —**Martin Ssemakula, Kampala, Uganda**

"Well, so many things in my mind. But I think our disorganization frustrates me most. In a nutshell, Africans' inability to think for the general good of [the] public is the most frustrating. Everyone thinks for himself and his own good, and that creates such confusion. I doubt we can ever have a collective voice. Find any unit [for example] a family and ask them how you can help them. All of a sudden they will disagree over everything and none will relent, even if it risks losing your help altogether. I cannot start telling you about how dirty and needlessly loud we are."—**Joseph Kabuleta, Kampala, Uganda**

"How much culture has permeated the African's psyche. Culture in Africa supersedes education and religion. Except the White South Africans perhaps. And the Algerians. Remember the Rumbek [Sudan People's Liberation Movement meeting] minutes? The Col. Dr. [John Garang] was [espousing] brilliant strategy one minute, and then superstitious garbage the next. And it's the same all over Africa." —**Amina Osman, Kampala, Uganda**

"Knowing the right thing but spending time [and] resources trying to do things wrongly." —**Dan Kasirye, Nairobi, Kenya**

"Taking people for granted. It's rare for anyone to ask if it's okay before they can make a decision that concerns man. Husbands, wives, kids, colleagues are all taken for granted." —**Irene Kiiza, Kampala, Uganda**

"[L]ife dictators and senile presidents leading brilliant people." —**Joseph Beyanga, Kampala, Uganda**

"There is no escaping one thing. Wherever you go, Africans tend to live in desperate conditions. Socially, mentally, spiritually, and economically. Exceptions of course exist, but generally, something is lacking. And this is what leads me to my most general observation, which can be summed up in one word—mediocrity. Poor, or rich—even filthy rich—I find … it all too often rather too easy to attach that unflattering adjective to Africans." —**Moses Mwayle, Tokyo, Japan**

"How they survive in harsh environments and still continue to smile." —**Pamela Batenga, Kampala, Uganda**

"Their distinct lack of a curiosity about their origins and how they came to be where they are. Also, about their linguistic links to other Africans thousands of miles away. [Furthermore] the increasing loss of an age-old capacity to listen and engage in reasoned debate." —**Kalundi Robert Serumaga, Kampala, Uganda**

"Africans seem helpless about their problems and even those who fought for independence … found it convenient to re-colonize us … afresh, as in, preferring to carry on the exploitation. Our voice was taken away and matters are not helped when we globalize and [our] part-time thinking. Whites have to decide the how. Rwanda is lucky a whole generation did the exodus, giving way for a fresh start. Uganda's wars have not dismantled colonial structures. So the vicious cycle." —**Ebony Quinto, Kampala, Uganda**

"A typical African's daylong struggle of the rat race survival on less than a dollar, barefooted, hungry, sweating, stressed, no health insurance, all diseased but pays all allegiance to the hoisting of the national flag and de-hoisting of the same flag, day in, day out. The puzzling [thing] is that transformation stage from the subnormal state of mind, to the general population mindset, standing at attention [along] with everybody." —**Charles Kaijabwango, Kampala, Uganda**

"Perhaps what puzzles me about myself and fellow Africans is the naïve faith that we have the bite to claim the same position as the West in terms of global positioning, should we bring our minds together. Or should I say that we very much claim [to be] Africanist yet deep in our hearts we [admire] everything western." —**James Tamale, Kampala, Uganda**

"The thing that puzzles me about Africans is saying things they actually do not mean, the complete failure to correlate their minds with their speech, or conscience with what comes out of their mouths, makes me suspect quite a number of things about us and completely perplexes me. It is so difficult to judge an African on the basis of what he tells you, or claims to stand for, and therein lays the problem of IQ tests and studies conducted in Africa that rely on surveys; in other words, the African purveys a high level of irrationality even where his own interests as a creature are concerned." —**Arthur Musinguzi, Washington DC, USA**

"How we all see the problem and might know the solutions, but are not willing to work them out." —**Paul Amailuk, Melbourne, Australia**

"What puzzles me about Africans is the uniformity in all the countries ... [the] poor time keeping, there is always the feeling that time is on their side. Despite the opinion that colonialism or the western culture has swept away the traditional African culture, I think that Africans still honor some of their customs, whether they are good or bad. The most puzzling [thing] is when they make the better of two cultures. For instance the priest who has an ancestral shrine at home, the Christian who still visits a witchdoctor's shrine or keeps fetishes and talismans." —**Jan Annette Ajwang, Kampala, Uganda**

"Africans (and Africa as an entity) always have much promise, but that's always as far as it goes. It never materializes ... A weird thing is that Africans use foreign definitions exclusively for almost everything of theirs ... Many quirks, for certain. Too hospitable, yet ready to fight over a few paces of desert sand ... There seems to always be some unseen Force doing its best to keep Africans at the lower rungs. If it's not war, then bad economic policies. Not that? Try transport and communication. Not that? Something else, then. Always something. This is where I come close to believing that stuff about the curse." —**Revence Kalibwani, Entebbe, Uganda**

"Copying what someone already has [created]. No originality." —**Bonnie Agea, Dar es Salaam, Tanzania**

"It's our ordinariness." —**Nicholas Sengoba, Kampala, Uganda**

"What puzzles me most about Africans is our lack of self-esteem. We are happy to wallow in our own misery and to destroy all that is around us all the while blaming the colonialists who built the things that we are destroying. I am also disturbed by our low expectations of our leaders." —**David Mpanga, Kampala, Uganda**

"Answer to your question: justification and rationalization of the absurd. Protecting the corrupt, stolen elections, land vs. cruisers, medicine versus textbooks, wife inheritance, female genital mutilation, lack of personal responsibility for actions in and out of home." —**Nafula Awori, Kampala, Uganda**

"It is the way Africans perceive issues and fail to understand things in an African way and understand issues the western European way." —**Abraham Emong, Kampala, Uganda**

"Africans are intimidated [by] thinking. People do not want to think; they do not take time to think. The inability to plan and look ahead also puzzles me a lot. We have a lot of 'smart' people who went to western universities and even lived there awhile but when they come back home you do not seem to see the difference. You would think that some of the western sharpness would rub against them but somehow this critical aspect of thinking eludes the African!" —**Daniel Karibwije, Kigali, Rwanda**

"Our speed (we seem to be trained to be slow). We take life slow not fast like elsewhere, so, poor time keeping." —**Benjamin Mpeirwe, Kampala, Uganda**

"Their inferiority complex, the belief that we cannot do as good a job as guys from the West, or that we can't grasp concepts that they can." —**Ivan Musoke, Kampala, Uganda**

"I am puzzled by the African's hate of himself." —**Oscar Bamuhigire, Kampala, Uganda**

"The refusal to pursue the road to success even where the road is tested. The reluctance to emulate others who have succeeded before them." —**Patrick Luganda, Kampala, Uganda**

"Answering questions with questions, their unwillingness or inability to be meticulous, and their failure to keep time, most times. African time." —**Florence Kayemba, Port Harcourt, Nigeria**

"Contentment with mediocre standards." —**Elias Biryabarema, Kampala, Uganda**

"The fatalistic attitude that absolves the African from deciding his own destiny." —**George Okot, Kampala, Uganda**

"It's the way they laugh. Ugandans laugh so much, almost at everything for so long. I think I might be the one with no sense of humor!" —**Beti O. Kamya, Kampala, Uganda**

"Their lack of ambition." —**Godfrey Kyedza, Kampala, Uganda**

"For a reason that is not clear to me, we are so unfortunate … in many ways. And we are [so] defeated psychologically already that we are [too] crippled to do anything; I mean even the thing we can do. We are brain-washed in a negative way … We think, me me me, from the top down. … We don't think far … those of us who do, have a zillion obstacles … in general, we are so unfortunate." —**Kidist Gebreselassie, Virginia, USA**

"We have everything needed, resource-wise, to develop into first-world economies, but why do we still lag behind? Secondly it is obvious that the white man is intellectually superior to the African. What is the cause of this? Were we created that way by God? Isn't there anything we can do to improve our lot in terms of intellect?" —**Anthony Apiku, Entebbe, Uganda**

"Honestly, it's one of those tough questions but I must say, unfortunately, we seldom pay attention to detail … It's that folly of aversion to detail that confines many African countries to [a] never-ending state of confusion … about silly mistakes, about not being inquisitive, about taking things for granted, about taking orders as givens." —**Moses Khisa, Calcutta, India**

"With the exception of South Africa, the African countries I've visited are dirty, poor at keeping time (flights and so forth), and corrupt. In fact, we Africans appear resigned to mediocrity if not failure. Poor governance is bafflingly apparent everywhere." —**Mark Namanya, Kampala, Uganda**

"They all seem to take time for granted, who so and so dresses like this, marries the other, yet [make] no effort to stop what

affects them like corruption, abusive leaders, environmental degradation, etc. Even [in] Kenya [in 2007/08], it was a tribal question not a principle of good governance [or] democracy."
—**Sarah Nsigaye, Kampala, Uganda**

"Africans generally find it normal never to keep time. It puzzles and annoys me." —**Mariam Nakisekka, Kampala, Uganda**

"The stark, shameless manifestation of boorish self-interest of African rulers we call 'leaders'!" —**FDR Gureme, Kampala, Uganda**

"The lack of shared values. Some sacrifice, others are in church. Some are in Kololo [an upscale residential district of Kampala], others in hovels and huts … Chaos!" —**Joseph Ntiro, Kampala, Uganda**

"What strikes me most is that the African [is] puzzled about being African! Most answers point to what exactly makes an African: lazy, dirty, unserious, little interest in education, especially further education, no sense of time, etc. If that's what makes an African, why do we want to change it? Why are we surprised or puzzled by this? I spent many years in Europe, living like a high middle-class European, but my instinct was always to get back to Africa to live like an African. An African will always get fed up with keeping time all the time, with working so hard that every task is completed, with reading something constructive and educative every day (other than gossip in the newspapers!). I did … and others are making that great decision of coming back to Africa right now, abandoning highly [sought after] lucrative jobs. Why? To live the African dream and I mean dreaaaaam." —**John Katto, Kampala, Uganda**

"Their [inability] to adapt, change, modify their lifestyle. As in, you take a girl to Rome, you are dining out and pasta is the norm for dinner and she asks for matoke [a staple Ugandan dish made from bananas]. We are unique!" —**Denise Akii-Bua, United Kingdom**

"I tell you what really puzzles me these days. Mugabe! He's still here! He has single-handedly destroyed a prosperous nation. He thinks printing more money will somehow solve the economic crisis. And, he almost won re-election! He took his sweet time announcing his defeat, and then promptly made it impossible to hold a re-run. What happened next? He became president again! And the victor? He became prime minister and widower to boot within a matter of months. And Mugabe's peers? They looked on sheepishly and made incoherent sounds about Zimbabweans being best placed to solve their internal problems. Could this really be a true modern-day story? Regrettably, it's an African one." —**Ebert Byenkya, Kampala, Uganda**

"What puzzles me about Africans is deference without accountability. We defer to others based on wealth, office, social status, and race without question … The other things are apathy and opportunism." —**Simon Sebaggala, London, United Kingdom**

"Generally good people and too trusting. We do not ask questions even when they are necessary." —**Stephen Batanda, Kampala, Uganda**

"[The] love for shortcuts to everything." —**Joel Isabirye, Kampala, Uganda**

"I am puzzled by the very strange way we have failed to 'sell' and also uphold our values/knowledge/histories, geographies from within our 'localities' and so easily accept what others have thought of us." —**Ronald Muwambi, Dubai, United Arab Emirates**

"What puzzles me about Africans is the lack of humility and poor marketing skills. It puzzles me how Africans can brag even after they commit inhumane offences [against] people they are supposed to protect. African leaders are very good at this. About marketing, we Africans have lots of hidden talents and skills but we are very poor at showing that we are good at anything." —**Isaac Mutenyo, London, United Kingdom**

"At this point, the fact that there is no end in sight for the suffering and no room for true democracy and so forth." —**Merawit Biadghlign, Seattle, USA**

"What puzzles me about Africans is our lack of accountability. We are known for creating problems, but failing to own them." —**Sandra Luba, Los Angeles, USA**

"[In Ethiopia and Zambia and other African countries] … It is the same disorganization of management by crisis, where there is so much time to organize [events], moreover things that don't cost money, but at the last minute [nothing has been done]." —**Jude Kagoro, Kampala, Uganda**

I have included this chapter in this book simply to help you form an unbiased opinion of your own and understand why Africa and Africans have remained in a state of backwardness. The responses above are not my own words, and I would protest owning them. But I simply did not want you to take part 1 of "What Has Caused Africa to Remain in a State of Backwardness" as being the view of one individual, your author. Therefore, chapter 3 offers you opinions from other Africans of why they think the continent is in a state of backwardness. Some of the responses given above are discussed in the next chapters, and I hope you will fully appreciate my analysis.

Chapter Four

⤳

Removing Backwardness in Africa

*If tradition was backwardness, then development would have to
be induced … as to remove backwardness and fight tribalism,
all in the name of development.*
                                                        —Mahmood Mamdani[9]

The very unfortunate thing is that many people do not spend
much time asking how human society has developed. Perhaps
they do not know much about this subject, because you hear
different theories about it. In my African language, Lusoga,
a very rich language with quite a few confusing cultural
underpinnings, we have a number of descriptions for a child as
he or she grows. If the child is just born, a few days to around two
months, this child is called *Akhaweere*. When the child develops
the first tooth at between four and six months, that child will be
called *Omwanha*. Across all levels of development—when the
child is crawling, standing, and walking—all these stages have
some sort of culture-centric descriptions in the Kisoga culture.
The child is called *Omwanha* until puberty—and beyond by
his or her parents. Right now, I am known to my parents as
Omwanha. During puberty, a boy child is called *Omulenzi*

and a girl, *Omuwala*. When the boy grows into a man, he is called *Omusadha*, and when an old man, he is called *Muzei*. Similarly, society is said to undergo stages of development. What confuses me about my own culture, the Basoga, is that the *Omwanha* will always be *Omwanha* in the presence of his or her parents. This is very profound and shows great respect for the parents. But the phrase represents a backward way of referring to the adult *Omwanha*, because this *Omwanha* will always expect his or her parents to reason for him or her until that time when they are deceased. Many adult orphans, not only among the Basoga but also among other tribes across the African continent, cannot do a single thing for themselves because they were never subjected to reason and creativity when growing up. They are simply living in the *Omwanha attitude* as the Basoga would want it to be.

Regardless of the above, we must be able to describe the development of society like the Basoga described the development of a human being. We should not baby-sit societies just because the parents, who are the leaders in this case, are still living. It is true that the problem with some African leaders is that they are unable to comprehend that society goes through stages. This is why they are not able to provide solutions. For instance, let's focus on the *Musoga* man (*Omusadha*); how should *Omusadha* be? We can answer this by describing the subject of modernization; modernization is assumed to be the mature stage of society. We have at least six major fundamentals of a modern society:

1. Full employment or near full employment
2. Factors of production that are efficiently utilized—i.e., land, labor, capital, and entrepreneurship being

fully and efficiently in use (this is illustrated in graphs A and B). We cannot get to this stage outside the realm of industrialization, because countries that have industrialized have also modernized.

3. Modernized services such as transport, banks, insurance, hotels, and tourism not only flourish; they are in place as support services to the modernization plans of an economy.

4. Education and research are well developed and are always checked to ensure they are efficiently meeting the needs of a modernizing economy.

5. Property rights and ownership—modernized societies have laws and regulations to guarantee ownership of property by citizens. Citizens exercise the freedom within the prevailing laws to acquire and dispose off property without a lot of constraints. Such a society is also characterized by a vibrant citizenship, which is creative and innovative.

6. Free movement of commerce—besides the freedom to own property, citizens exercise creative means of transacting business within and outside their economies on a daily basis.

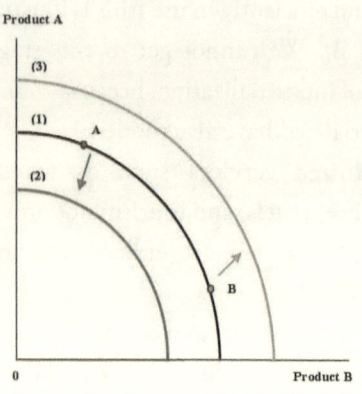

Graph A

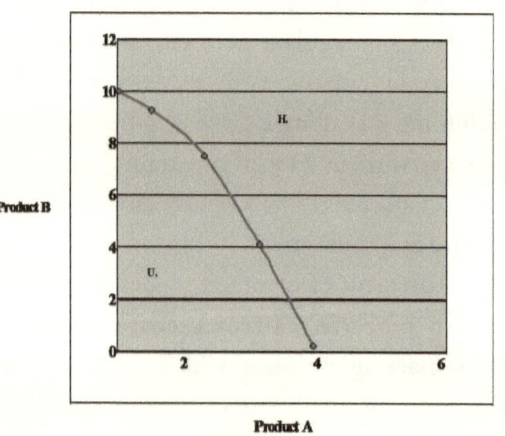

Graph B

Above are production possibilities frontier curves (PPF) to compare production engagements in both developed and developing nations, assuming production based on two products, i.e. Product A (consumer good) and Product B (capital good).

Graph A represents a fully developed economy that has the capacity to produce on any of the curves 1, 2, and 3. The difference is that for the economy to grow from 1 to 3 there must be an improvement in technology leading to that growth. Most Western economies have that kind of growth because their technology is fully developed, and they are able to employee most if not all their resources (i.e., land, labor, capital, and entrepreneurship). On the other hand, if a developed country shifted from 1 to 2, we could say that it was losing some of its growth potential and unemployment rates were rising as a result of some bad economic conditions, like the recent economic crisis in the United States.

Further, most developing nations, with the majority in Africa, are engaged in production based on graph B. Specifically, these countries are simply engaged in backward productive means (i.e., they are using poor technology, they lack fertilizers, and they rarely employee any scientific means in the production process). They are found to produce at point U. This point represents inefficient production, whereby not all the country's resources are employed. It is unlikely that most African countries have attained conditions that can enable them to produce at point H (point of economic growth). What all this means is that African countries especially must focus their attention on developing or embracing technology that can enable them to achieve efficient production and yield economic growth.

To elaborate further, land, in economic terms, does not mean only what we walk on every day; it also means all natural resources—minerals, forests, water, etc. Secondly, labor refers to human beings who can efficiently utilize their mental and physical abilities to produce goods and services to sustain consumption. But we should not invest more in the means of consumption than in the means of production. The two should go hand in hand. Third, capital means stored value. This value could be in the form of machinery, factories, etc; it is not money alone, as some people want to think. For instance, if I worked in the past and bought a motorcycle with my earnings, that motorcycle is a capital item, because I can use it to do other things. For instance, many East Africans have resorted to using motorcycles as a means of transportation to earn a living. The same is equally applicable to a tractor that I can use to cultivate the land before I grow any crops. Suppose I do not buy any capital equipment and only keep the money in the bank; that money is earning interest for me and that also constitutes capital. Most Africans have very poor saving tendencies; this is because most of if not all income earned is sufficient only to meet consumption needs with little or none to invest. The poor saving culture is explained by the high cost of living and the dependence ratio in families. Regardless of these constraints, the need to save has not fully sunk into the economies of Africa. In the next paragraphs, I explain some basic savings models, which I hope can work for many of our people in Africa.

The saving model is constructed as follows. Income *(Y)* minus Consumption *(C)* is equal to Savings or $S = Y - C$. Many people, including Africans, do not know that when we consume a bit of our income, what remains is savings. Savings *(S)* times the number of years for which you have saved that money *(x years)* —if placed in an interest-bearing account at a banking institution—is equal to investment *(I)*. $(S) * (x years) = I$; where S is savings, x is the number of years savings are kept in the bank, and I is investment.

Personal consumption in economics means expenditure on yourself and not spending on productive activities.

Consumption for oneself would include buying food, clothing, leisure items, etc. More precisely, we have two kinds of consumption according to Marx (in George Ritzer (2005) "subsistence and luxury consumption." Subsistence consumption takes the form of buying basic foodstuffs and other home-based commodities. Conversely, luxury consumption is when individuals are engaged in buying for elegance, for example, expensive automobiles. Therefore, income minus what you consume in those various ways leaves your savings. If you save for a number of years, you will be able to invest. Today, most economies are growing as a result of too much consumption whether by subsistence or luxury means. In the case of Africa, this consumption is mainly for survival and not for enjoying life. We must move away from this kind of consumption.

In order to better estimate the influence of income on consumption, we need to take the initiative to understand any influences that flow from consumption to income. This can be analyzed in the deeper and more complex economic models for better understanding. But when these economic models are used, the relationship between consumption and disposable income is weakened only a little. Thus, disposable income remains the major determinant of consumption spending, yet it is not the only thing that may matter. In ignoring this finding, many economists have tended to give poor advice by asserting that the correlation between consumption and income results exclusively from the effects of income on consumption. Many economists, for that matter, have come to conclude that the income-expenditure model explains widely how the world works (i.e., autonomous and unexplainable consumptions). Unless an explanation of changes in investment from changes in income or financial conditions is provided, the income-expenditure model will be a partial and perhaps misleading way to view the world or simply our dear Africa.

The assumption that business investment should be sensitive to both interest rates and expectations of future earnings must also hold when explaining why people resort to consumption alone and ignore investing. The idea here is that interest rates for investment funds in Africa are unbearable, and such higher interest rates simply discourage business investments (i.e., making individuals resort to consuming their hard-earned incomes with no need to borrow extra and start some form of business). When talking about investments, the need for residential construction and changes in inventories is paramount. The time has not yet come for many individuals in Africa to realize that their residential constructions will one day result in an investment. These forms of investment respond to financial conditions and total spending, though not in the same ways as business investments. As with consumption, changes in investment may react to changes in the economy with a time lag. Therefore, we should state that Africans in most countries are currently experiencing an investment lag, which might be caused by any of the following: 1) high interest rates, which do not attract business investment; 2) fear of the unknown in future income or earnings or failure to take risks; 3) high family dependency ratios (something that is largely expected in culture-centric communities like those of Africa; 4) lack of political will or patriotism; 5) an inadequate education system whose outcome is workers and not creators of work; and 6) effects of post-colonialism as revealed in the high dependency on foreign donations in the form of material, money, and ideas by the poor countries.

If these issues are tackled as problems affecting the African continent and its population, then Africa will develop an investment culture to be sustained for a much longer period of time.

Further, emphasis should be placed on the fact that capital is past savings that have been invested. For instance, a young man who invests his little income to buy a bicycle or motorcycle for business purposes has reason to celebrate the value of investing. In this case, the bicycle or motorcycle represents a capital item as a result of investment. The young man can then use the bicycle or motorcycle to carry *Matooke* (green bananas or plantains) to the market where he can earn more money. If the bicycle is used in that way, the Basoga call it *okusubula* (doing business). If the bicycle is used to carry milk from the farm for family consumption, it will be an item of consumption; in this way, the *Musoga* will not have done business but used the capital item to efficiently provide for his family.

By full employment of factors of production, I mean all the factors should be working and not be left idle. Take the case of the Ugandan region called Karamoja, a region known for the worst backwardness in the history of Uganda; one wonders whether this region is fully employed or utilized. In the recent past, the region was characterized by the following: large pieces of land, forests, human beings, and cows, but guess what. One can regard all these Karamajong assets to be fully engaged in deep sleep! If they were not, their cattle would be much healthier than they are today. A fully grown and well-fed indigenous cow should weigh about 250 kilograms (550 pounds), but because it has worms, it is undervalued. The Karamajong region inherited these situations because nothing was considered to exercise full potential for economic exploit. I have only used the Karamajong region as an example, but in the larger contexts of the African continent, we still have many communities sharing the same characteristics as the Karamajong.

The above description is characteristic of most backward countries, especially the underutilization of the factors of production: labor and natural resources. People are just sitting at home. For instance, many tribes in Africa spend quite a great deal of time greeting, *"Mmhh, Osiibye otya nno? Maamu, Nyooge etc?"* The whole day is spent on greeting. Why? It is because time management is not a priority, and this is a backward mentality. We should stop wasting valuable time in noneconomic activities. It's universal respect to greet one another, but it should not take two people very much time to greet each other each time they meet in a single day. Even Africans who have migrated to the Western world are still being held behind on time management, except those working in the Western corporate culture, but this is only because they are working for somebody else who happens to be of a different culture and values production time. Most important to note is that Africans in the Diasporas are fond of showing up late for their own functions—whether they be church, weddings, funerals, or graduation ceremonies. Regardless of the reason, time wasted cannot be retrieved. A leading evangelist and teacher on leadership, Bishop David Oyedepo[10] argues "that time is too precious to be invested in watching people and events which make news." He further argues that he "is informed and believes it is ignorance which has kept Africa behind other continents." Furthermore, the bishop reasons that "those who make news do not watch news; but they expect other people to watch what they are doing! Time is too precious to be spent following what people do, instead of investing it in work." By not valuing time for effective, productive means, we are simply exercising backwardness in time management.

Consequently, where the whole society is operating at a very low pulse (i.e., where everything is done in a relaxed way and people take time to do a simple greeting), that society is simply backward. We have been branded backward because we cannot find the time for things that we value. On another note, modern cell phone technology is a very good development, but some of us Africans are yet to reap those benefits. The cell phone in Africa has improved business, but it has also brought a lot of problems. Analytically, I think these problems outweigh the marginal benefits the cell phones have provided Africa as a continent. The phones are often misused in so many nonproductive activities. Despite the biting poverty the people in Africa face, many Africans have managed to afford and possess as many as two phone handsets per head. Unfortunately, these phones have created more problems than they have solved. Whoever made the phone eased communication for many people, but cell phones in Africa are often clipped on one's pants in order that the whole world can see that one has a phone, or those who own more than one line have gone to the extent of using at least one line for mischief. This mischief takes the form of planning and executing robberies and other such immoral behaviors. Even if not used for such activities, people use the phones to talk endlessly as if there were no productive engagements for them to take on. Conversely, in order to modernize, we must fully or nearly fully, utilize land, labor, capital (including our cell phones), and entrepreneurship in productive ventures.

Entrepreneurship entails the ability to detect economic opportunities and take advantage of them. Lack of entrepreneurial ability is one of the problems of most backward countries. Backward communities rarely see opportunities, let alone take advantage of them. One example of such an opportunity I can give here pertains to the abundant crocodiles in the numerous lakes and rivers of Africa that have lived there for generations. I have been told that some time ago, in the early 1990s, some white men from Zimbabwe and one Ugandan, Dr. Alex Babitunga (now deceased), started a crocodile ranch and turned it into an enterprising firm called Uganda Crocs Limited (UCL). The crocodiles were slaughtered for skin and meat export. In the beginning, one kilogram of crocodile meat cost 12,000 Ugandan shillings or $5.40 in today's U.S. dollars. One pair of men's shoes made of crocodile skin was going for not less than 900,000 Ugandan shillings ($402.68) and a pair of women's for 600,000 Ugandan shillings ($268.46). A belt with mere patches of crocodile leather was going for 90,000 Ugandan shillings ($40.27).

This is a very good example of entrepreneurial opportunity. Crocodiles have been in Uganda living with Ugandans for a very long time, and they have been eating our relatives for years. But no single Ugandan in his single-minded head ever considered whether he could use the crocodiles, which were eating people, in an economic way until the white man came and said that there could be a lot of money in these crocodiles if A, B, C, and D were done. Indeed, the strong handbags that our African ladies love so much and the classic leather shoes are often made out of strong crocodile skin! What is funny and backward in reality is that these leather items are made outside of Africa, yet the raw material is from this continent. The other amazing part of this is that none of the African people ever saw the opportunity I have just described above until the white men from Zimbabwe came and made money out of that opportunity, which millions of Ugandans had not seen. My question is why should the white man have to show us our own opportunities? This only tells us that the level of entrepreneurship in most black Africans is very low because of the pre-Capitalist culture and low education.

In view of our myopic attitude to taking advantage of our own natural resources, how can we fully employ our people? The solution here is industrialization; the more industries you build, the more people you will be able to employ. Subsistence agriculture cannot employ many people. How many people do you need to dig half an acre using a hoe? Not many—two or three. This explains why there is a problem of employment in the backward countries. The nature of the activities being undertaken, such as subsistence agriculture, cannot provide enough jobs. Only industries can provide large numbers of sustainable jobs.

Consider small countries like Rwanda (which is about 27,000 square kilometers) and Burundi (about the same size). You can say that Rwanda and Burundi are about 50,000 square kilometers together. The two countries combined have a population of approximately fourteen million people. Most of the time, the news from Rwanda and Burundi report that these countries are overcrowded! Yet Holland, which has a land area of 40,000 square kilometers, is smaller than Rwanda and Burundi combined and has a population of sixteen million people. When you go to Holland, you do not even see the people! You find that in the countryside, there are no people; there are only farms. The people live in flats and work in the factories. In that small space in Holland, they are doing high-value work—producing computers, textiles, etc. In

Africa, however, where subsistence agriculture is prominent, one needs a big space to believe that he or she is engaged in production.

Countries like Rwanda and Burundi and most other African countries are considered overpopulated, but this is not true at all! They are simply underdeveloped, and their human potential is not developed either. The land output is very low because people are using poor seeds and no fertilizers. For instance, instead of one acre yielding eight tons of maize, a farmer will only realize 800 kilograms (a little more than 1600 pounds). Why is this? It is because most of our countries on the African continent have not set the basis for extensive farming. Extensive farming in Africa will require us to fully employ our resources by setting up industrialization corridors and positioning our countries for modernization. Our farmers must be educated on how to produce abundantly. They must be offered services like credit and access to fertilizers, seeds, tractors, and modern markets. Our road infrastructures must also be prepared and sustained to help farmers transport their products to export zones and centers.

The second element, which is a result of the first one, is widening the tax base, so that governments can collect taxes, support education and health care, build roads, and pay better salaries to public servants. Today, the United States, under President Barack Obama, is still grappling with whether they should offer public health care to Americans or leave the markets to take a toll on costs. When Congress, under a Democratic Party majority in both houses, voted to overhaul the health-insurance industry, those who did not agree with the idea went to court to stop the now health-care law from being implemented. This should not be happening in such a big and developed country like the United States. We Africans should be the ones dealing with the issue of determining whether public health care is more efficient than market-based care. It is an idea that provokes fights amongst economists with their contradicting theories, but in reality, it is a fundamental right for all human beings to live sound and healthy lives. If Africa is to invest in her citizens through good health to enhance productivity at this time, government-aided health care should take priority. Most of our citizens don't live beyond age fifty on average. In addition, our countries are experiencing quite a surge in the young populations. In fact, we have countries in Africa in which young people are half or more than half of the total population. We do not have time and money to debate the issue of public health care like the United States has been doing for decades. The United States is developed enough, and in my opinion, they can debate how the markets can control health care as long as they want. There are things worthy for the markets, but health care in backward Africa should be controlled by the governments as long as they are not corrupt. The other most important issue we should capitalize on is the creation of infrastructure for industrialization so that our healthy people can find work. The more industries you have, the more products they produce and the more tax you collect. If you tax many things, you will collect more money than if you tax only two crates of beer or Coca-Cola. We should get to a point at which the world is no longer divided into two types of countries: donor countries, which collect more tax than they need for themselves, and recipient countries, which receive aid because they do not collect enough tax and can only survive by getting donations from other countries (i.e., countries that collect more taxes than they need).

When Idi Amin of Uganda, in 1972, chased away the Indians, in what he termed an "economic war," as he said, "I am engaged in an economic war—I want the Africans to take control of their economy," he was simply exercising idiocracy as a leader. According to Amin, Africans were not controlling the economy in spite of the fact that they were exporting sugar, textiles, and beef, even though some of the market players were brown-colored. The most important part of the story to tell here is that when Amin gave the once Indian-owned shops to the Ugandans to operate after the Indians had left for Britain and other destinations, the shops dried out of any merchandise. Those Ugandans who became reapers of what they did not sow depleted the shops of the merchandise through selling and freely consuming of the goods without restocking. In the end, the once enterprising shops and towns of Uganda became a laughing stock. Shops were closed down, and the buildings were vandalized beyond repair. The end result was an economy with small black markets scattered across the country and a very small tax base that could not sustain government expenditures.

Further, Madhvani (of Uganda) is an Indian by descent, but he is more African than two million Africans combined because he is contributing more value to Africa. By producing sugar, soap, and a number of other products, Madhvani is instrumental in the productive activities of Uganda. On top of producing these products, he pays the government of Uganda close to thirty billion shillings annually in taxes.[11] This is equivalent to funding the entire Ugandan parliament for a month. On the other hand, British American Tobacco (BAT) pays the government of Uganda close to forty-five billion U.S. dollars as tax.[12] This is enough money to fund the operations of over thirty districts in Uganda, if the problem of corruption is curtailed. On top of what BAT, Madhvani, and other foreign-owned companies pay to the government, they are also employers to many Ugandan families, whom they pay monthly salaries. These individual families use the salaries to pay their bills and send their children to school. BAT, like many other foreign-based companies (see figure 5 for the firms paying the most taxes in Uganda) pays for electricity consumption and other services to remain in operation. What these factories are doing is simply sustaining the Ugandan economy. Similar scenarios are widely present in many other African countries. Therefore, African countries only need to industrialize to sustain their economies.

No.	TOP TAXPAYERS, 2005/2006 TAXPAYER	Ownership (F = Foreign, D = Domestic, D/F(both)	Total (billions of UgShs.
1	M.T.N. UGANDA LIMITED	F	120,014,563,759
2	SHELL UGANDA LTD.	F	105,505,602,349
3	UGANDA BREWERIES LTD	D	70,055,233,294
4	NILE BREWERIES LTD	D	49,593,222,491
5	CALTEX OIL (U) LTD	F	47,460,645,952
6	TOTAL UGANDA LIMITED.	F	46,207,073,913
7	BAT UGANDA 1984 LIMITED.	F	45,407,569,783
8	CENTURY BOTTLING CO. LTD.	F	43,737,951,033
9	TORORO CEMENT INDUSTRIES LIMITED	D	35,258,707,394
10	STANBIC BANK (U) LTD.	F	33,206,283,732
11	PETROCITY ENTERPRISES	F	30,704,654,877
12	UGANDA TELECOM LIMITED	D	30,632,184,771
13	KAKIRA SUGAR WORKS (1985) LTD	F	29,019,600,430
14	PETRO UGANDA LIMITED	F	28,047,625,929
15	HIMA CEMENT FACTORY LTD	D/F	24,901,976,648
16	ROOFINGS LTD	D/F	23,078,432,017
17	GAPCO UGANDA LTD.	D/F	21,431,514,773
18	KINYARA SUGAR WORKS LTD	D/F	21,181,946,712
19	AGGREKO INTERNATIONAL PROJECTS LIMITED	F	20,855,283,730
20	KOBIL UGANDA LIMITED	F	20,453,341,346
21	UMEME LIMITED	F	19,118,899,265
22	STANDARD CHARTERED BANK UGANDA LIMITED	F	18,500,173,605
23	MINISTRY OF FINANCE AN	D	17,693,918,694
24	HASS PETROLEUM (U) LTD (EFCO OIL)	F	16,409,376,689
25	HARED PETROLEUM LIMITED	F	15,306,235,247
26	ELECTORAL COMM.	D	14,620,870,677
27	BARCLAYS BANK (U) LTD.	F	13,995,576,246
28	UGANDA REVENUE AUTHORITY	D	13,862,686,541
29	HASHI EMPEX LTD	F	13,643,346,800
30	MAKERERE UNIVERSITY COUNCIL	D	13,447,151,576
31	SUGAR CORPORATION OF UGANDA LIMITED	F	12,341,052,305
32	DELTA PETROLEUM LIMITED	F	11,764,280,655
33	CELTEL (U) LTD	F	11,244,121,672
34	A.K. OILS AND FATS (U) LIMITED	F	10,984,582,924
35	MUKWANO INDUSTRIES (U) LTD	D	10,414,905,487
36	NAT WATER & SEW CORP A/C VARIOUS	D	10,214,304,522

Source: New Vision, Monday, August 7, 2006

Figure 5

**Table showing some of the corporations
paying the most tax in Uganda**

The companies represented in the table paid over ten billion Ugandan shillings in the 2005–2006 tax year to the government of Uganda. What is surprising is that out of thirty-six firms, fourteen of them are either completely or partially domestically owned. The rest of the firms are foreign-owned—meaning that Uganda as a nation (like many African nations) is very much dependant on these foreign-based companies for tax revenue, employment for citizens, direct investments to spur economic growth, and other social responsibilities. What leaders have failed to do is create programs that stimulate domestic investments to counter the direct investment domination of foreign firms in terms of business ownership. Such investment is not necessarily a bad thing because the economy does grow, but to what extent are Africans in charge of their own economic growth and development? When will Africans ever own businesses in large numbers and act as employers of fellow Africans?

The third major element is the development of Africa's human resources through education and accessible health care. What do we mean by "developing the human resources"? Africa has very wonderful and beautiful people. They are human beings, but have they developed their potential? We should turn our sons and daughters into creative human beings who not only report to work but also create work in industries. By creating work, I mean, our people need to move beyond being looked at only as job seekers and become job makers. Governments should be more proactive in creating an environment conducive to creative minds thriving in modernization. If we do not modernize, we shall perish.

You must have heard that there were people called Indians in America; they were the owners of that land. Where are they now? When we say "Americans," we do not mean American Indians. We mean descendents of the people who came and pushed out the former inhabitants who were less modernized. They were very courageous in a primitive way. The gun, which is a product of the mind, was used to chase them away. Therefore, when the human resources are not developed, they will be stuck in one place; in the end, it can result in slavery, or worse, extermination. There is no parking slot for fools in the world. No one is going to say, "This one is a fool. Let us allot him his slot until two hundred years from now."

One requirement for modernization, therefore, is education for all. People must all go to school and stay there long enough to learn new skills and new attitudes. And, of course, they need to be healthy. If they are infected with worms, for instance, how will they perform? You cannot educate them sustainably without considering all of the above factors. I am always appalled to read stories about striking students in African universities—moreover that most of these students strike for very minor reasons; for example, some students strike because their registration fees have been increased marginally, which does not happen every year. Others strike because of the bad food ... you name it. Any students anywhere pursuing an education must value themselves as raw material under process. Raw materials never strike; instead, they are thrown out of the process if they are bad for transformation into finished products. Similarly, universities in Africa whose students strike often need to do two things: 1) set the policies straight and communicate to the students well in advance and 2) be on the look out to eliminate noncomplying students as far as the policies set are concerned. Universities must be used to transform students into skilled individuals whose ethical tempers are worthy to represent them anywhere in the world.

A country like Japan has no oil. On the other hand, Saudi Arabia has a lot of oil. If we compare the Saudi and the Japanese people, we can see that the Japanese, who have neither oil nor minerals nor agricultural land, were the second most powerful economy in the world after the United States of America, until recently when China took over. Why? It is because they developed their human resources through education. Research has shown that Japan has the best developed human resources in the entire world. That is the reason they produce many of the machines used throughout the world—especially for us, the Africans, who produce none of the radios, computers, televisions, bicycles, or cars. These are the products of developed human resources. Secondly, what have the Arabs done to take advantage of the liquids in the ground, which were put there by somebody else? Are the Arabs the ones who put the oil in the ground? They simply have an established human resource to exploit that oil. Oil has been discovered in quite a number of places in Uganda and in other African nations, but these countries simply have no human resources capable of developing that oil into its useful form. The president of Uganda has been trotting the globe looking for oil scientists, engineers, and institutions that can train Ugandans to exploit their oil simply because the country does not have effective human resources to do the job. I must also state that the country is blessed with one of the best universities on the continent (i.e., Makerere University); however, for years, the engineers this university has produced are only occupying office space in the capital of Kampala, waiting for assignments from their line ministries. They simply cannot do anything under the power of their own brains. The country is losing quite a number of people in motor-vehicle accidents as a result of the narrow and poorly maintained roads, yet the engineers who can redesign and make better roads remain seated, just like everybody else. Parliament is also sitting around as though nothing is happening in the country that would prompt members to pass bills, such as those that can protect people on the roads. As Africans, we only require audacity to get changes in our state of affairs.

Let's look at the Democratic Republic of Congo (DRC) as another example. It is laughable for people to call the DRC a rich country. Rich? This is not a true statement. Some people have said that the DRC is rich because God put some minerals in the ground of that country. But the people in the same country are eating frogs, monkeys, you name it, and they cannot even produce enough food for subsistence because of wars and backward thinking within the population. Where is the wealth of the Democratic Republic of Congo? A rich country has skilled people. If you do not have skilled people, you have no riches. Therefore, Congo is simply backward, and it will not be rich until her human resources are developed to exploit the minerals in the ground.

The other aspect that is critical to address is the issue of markets. Once you have produced something, where will you sell it? Who will buy it from you? These are the issues Africans do not address often; the thinking "I will produce something, and whoever wants it will buy it" is backward thinking. You must ask yourself one question before you produce anything. Where is the market for what I am about to produce? Secondly, when we all produce the same thing, we are likely to find no market for the products, because each of us has the same product. It is very common for Africans to copy from each other; our minds have not been programmed to create anything on our own except children. This is something we can do well. But the idea of copying even follows Africans who migrate into the Western world. It is common for Africans in the Diasporas to copy from each other. If your friends work in a nursing home or own a certain type of business, your mind is not tuned to think in any way but to try to do exactly what your friends are doing. It is therefore unfortunate and indeed a shame that the curse of backwardness traces Africans regardless of where they live.

Furthermore, in typical Africa, our populations are small and only a small proportion stay in towns; the larger percentage live in villages. The one who is in the village will not buy from his neighbor, because most likely, the neighbor has similar products. There are no internal markets in most African communities, because more people stay in the rural areas than in urban areas. There is complementarity in production associated with the people in the rural areas. This is what makes us different from other societies, for instance, Europe, where the majority of the people live in urban areas and the minority in the villages. We should be producing for these Europeans who live in cities and have no villages to produce what we are able to produce. The main problem is that people who live in villages simply have no markets. When they produce extensively, governments must be there to help them market their produce. Villagers survive by subsistence and buy very little; they produce their own food and buy only textiles, paraffin, soap, and salt. This is backward. They should be given incentives to produce for the markets.

We should not forget that Europeans first colonized us and made us their markets. That is how they solved the question of the markets. They colonized India and established that country as their market. When the international community would not allow the keeping of colonies any longer, they formed the European Union, or the European market. The European Union market is approximately U.S. $8 trillion. The American market is approximately U.S. $15 trillion in GDP measures. The whole African market, if it was united, would be half a trillion dollars. These figures should mean something to us Africans. They should encourage us to focus on the idea of unifying our talents to make the continent of Africa the center for trade in this world.

What is surprising in our own Africa today is that we cannot sell products easily across the colonial borders. When you try to sell something in Kenya, Sudan, or Tanzania, they will tell you that it is another country and moreover a sovereign country. You insist you want to do some business there, but you are barred because it is another country. Africa is rich in republics, but also rich in poverty. It is rich in republics, presidents, ministers, MPs, and generals, but poor in development. Consequently, the lack of markets is a big problem that must be resolved or the continent will remain backward. I recently read in the papers that China supplied laptops to Rwanda in the name of donating to enhance computer literacy in that country. What the Rwandese government does not know is that China is simply testing its new computers on Rwandese children; once these computers pass the test, the Rwandese people will buy them. This notion not only stunts the minds of the young Rwandese children, preventing them from developing the ability to be creative and make their own computers when they grow up; it also creates and escalates a dependency syndrome in technology that has made Africa backward.

Another scenario that I think is of a backward nature is the Kenyan government's move to replace its ministers' durable cars with the Passat from Volkswagen, a German car manufacturer. Despite the hills the country has, the government expects its ministers to use these small vehicles to mobilize people for development. A Passat in America is a shopping or commuter vehicle used for traveling from home to work. It is not a business vehicle. The idea that government is saving fuel and high maintenance costs on the usual durable executive vehicles is backward. What the government of Kenya should have done was make its ministers be accountable for the classy vehicles. These vehicles must be used only for official duties. Needless to say, the move boosted the world auto industry; it had gone under, and the millions of dollars the Kenyans paid for the Passats have helped save the industry by a big margin.

Therefore, in order to solve the issue of markets within our disintegrated markets, we must integrate them. The East African Community, which has five countries today (i.e., Burundi, Kenya, Rwanda, Tanzania, and Uganda) promises to set an example for the rest of Africa if these countries fully integrate and even politically unify. Integrations provide strong foundations for developing countries, like those in Africa, to mingle in the global economy by reinforcing their bargaining power and increasing their "development space"[13] so that they can diversify and upgrade policies that guarantee alternative economic empowerment strategies. By the above argument, we need three movements on the question of markets. First, we must integrate the African market. Second, we must transform our societies into producers. Third, we should gain access to the rich European and American markets and others like the Chinese and Indian ones to market to them what we produce.

Chapter Five

The Need for Ideological Development

There is the need to embark upon a search and journey for an ideology that derives from our life and culture, from our political experience and our environment, and can thus relate to them. Something that is practicable in our unique political, economic, and social condition.

—Prince Charles Dickson[14]

There are many forms of political ideologies that can solve national problems. But before any ideologies are imported into Africa, Africans deserve the opportunity to Africanize themselves. By Africanizing, I mean accepting who we are, what we have, and what we have lived for since time immemorial (i.e., our cultures, norms, values, and all forms of the many African beliefs and rights as we surely know them) and avoid copying wholesale from the Western world. This understanding will bring us to realize what our problems are, which we must know before we can catch up with the rest of the world. Moreover, we need to develop confidence in ourselves as Africans so as to address and solve those problems that affect our continent most. We should not fear any retribution from donors or developmental partners because we have taken up what is right for Africa and Africans and shunned what is considered foreign. It is true the world is slowly becoming a global village; there are things that will not change whether in the West or in Africa. For instance, some of our cultural beliefs will not change.

Given the above understanding, we should note that our problems do have solutions of our own and not just those of outsiders who observe our affairs. It is okay to accept the advice and constructive criticism of our observers or what most technocrats have termed "development partners." But the solutions these people offer should be supplemental to our own. We owe ourselves the creation of modern states with strong democratic institutions manifested with our beliefs to safeguard those interests that we cherish. Moreover, our states should be built on the cornerstone of those very issues that we know are binding us as nations (ideological inclinations). We need to build our states on those ideas that matter to us most. On top of our ideas, we should emphasize how best our leaders can represent and be in a position to change the lives of their people, so they can be productive and constructive citizens. A developed country like the United States did not only prosper as a result of increased work productivity, but it also rightly condemned individuals who were not constructive citizens—or simply put, individuals who did not value work.

As John Kenneth Galbraith[15] points out in his book *The Economics of Innocent Fraud*:

In the UNITED STATES and, if less so, in other of the developed countries, no individuals invite as much criticism as those who escape the obligation to work. They are lazy, irresponsible, a burden—simply no good. This condemnation becomes severe when the alternative is public support. Nothing is publicly ... as unacceptable as going from work to welfare.

African leaders must learn from the above contribution that citizens of that continent must not be made or sustained on welfare—or be public good consumers only—instead, they must be developed through adequate educational initiatives and skills to attain minds of creativity and productivity. One pastor friend of mine from Rwanda once preached to a congregation I attended in Irving, Texas. Part of his sermon was geared toward leaders (at all levels) including pastors, who lead their people in survival tactics as opposed to revival tactics. By survival, he meant to say that there are leaders whose main goal is to create societies that survive only on their leadership (i.e., through dependency in all aspects of life). This type of leadership only manifests a state of backwardness. It will not help to revitalize true creativity and productivity in the African continent. Additionally, the revival style of leadership, from the pastor's perspective, meant that leaders were to redeem their people by paving ways and means to enable them to venture out and discover on their own what can sustain their lives. This kind of leadership suggests that African leaders should institute programs, build infrastructure, and enable environments that citizens can take advantage of and thrive in to better their lives—without necessarily depending on the welfare programs of governments and foreign donors. That said; leaders must not constitute themselves into pillars of all responsibility. In many African countries, leaders—oftentimes presidents—have found themselves solving village-based issues or problems. The leadership triangle in figure 6 illustrates strategies not only for organizations but also governments across Africa to emulate.

The Leadership Triangle

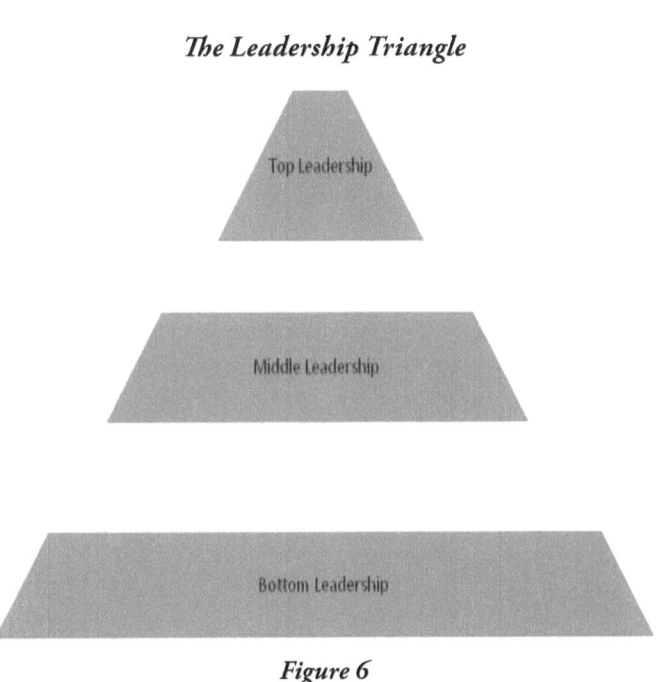

Figure 6

1. The bottom leadership—This represents those with the majority of responsibilities any institution has. This is where basic problems like who should handle accountability responsibilities for a health institution must be managed. It is also a level where skills matter; this level requires individuals who have gone to school or technical institutions to amass knowledge

and skills to enable institutional functions to work. This kind of leadership also calls for both basic and complex management skills to handle a group of employees from all walks of life while maintaining the proper functioning of the organization in an ethical manner.

2. The middle leadership—This level of leadership can also be referred to as the transactional leadership. The transactional leader often uses *management by exception*, working on the principle that if something is operating and can be defined as (and hence expected to be) performing, then it does not need attention. Exceptions to expectation require intervention: praise and reward for exceeding expectation and corrective action for performance that is below expectation. In the African context, this kind of leadership should be displayed at the head of the institutions, whether public or private. Public servants, like permanent secretaries, heads of parastatals, and inspector generals of government chiefs must take the role of transactional leadership. This is because they will combine skills, strategy, and leadership to get the work done. They must also be in a position to build long-lasting institutions, institutions that can outlive them, as opposed to building cocoons from which they, their relatives, and their friends can make a living.

3. The top leadership—This is where certain decisions must be made—decisions concerning issues that are national in nature or those that would be made at the top of any institutional leadership. We can simply say that this type of leadership must be transformational,

given the nature of the African continent. For example, those who should guide constructive legislation in parliament and eventually propel good and packaged bills into law must be found at this level. Presidents of our dear African nations need to stop handling petty matters, those that are not of national significance. A president cannot be in all places at all times but must learn how to delegate power to competent citizens— not his cronies, because by using his or her henchmen, the president is breeding corruption. It is important to note that as one transitions from the middle to top leadership, a lot of strategy is necessary.

All the same, what is surprising is that most leaders on the African continent, especially presidents, avoid delegating powers; instead, they assign the majority of state responsibilities to themselves. This idea delays a lot of important decisions that would have been made at the top of the triangle if leaders had not failed to delegate to the leadership at the bottom. This is not the way leadership should be organized, and it is happening in Africa. This backward practice should be rendered obsolete and changed for the betterment of the continent. Most important to note is that the triangle above embodies a systematic way of approaching leadership through delegation. As you move from the bottom base to the tip of the triangle, you should be able to recognize that responsibilities for leaders keep shrinking in number but growing in complexity.

Consequently, the top leadership—the president of a nation or the head of a public institution—should make the most complex decisions, which should be relatively few in number. The base of the triangle should be represented by positions occupied by individuals who are skilled in the technicalities of solving problems for the common man at any level in the institution. Such individuals should be economists, accountants, clerks, etc.

What Ideology Will Not Do

Despite the various forms of ideology, it is important to understand that our ideologies have limitations. Yes, they unify us and bind us into nations that share common beliefs, but they cannot address the facts on the ground—for instance, our backward thinking instincts and actions. Ideologies are not "fact-based." By fact-based, I mean what we are lacking, the experience to handle the challenges we face as we develop our nations. Ideologies should not assume the role of promoting policy exploitation by politicians or our leaders across different dimensions. Facts are based on the needs for the most people; ideologies are in place to create patriotism in us and foster our sense of nationalism for advancement as nations. Therefore, crafting policy initiatives based on ideology is failing to make a distinction between facts and ideologies.

For instance, the ideology that harbors the belief that Wall Street, Uganda Stock Exchange (USE), and Kenya Stock Exchange (KCE) executives have the expertise to manage and foster the functions of the World Bank or a nation's financial resources is one case in point where facts are at cross-purposes with ideology. It's now a common phenomenon for the World Bank to place former Wall Street executives into positions of responsibility in the bank. The main objective of the World Bank is development; it's not about creating financial instruments and monitoring their returns to investment. This is what Wall Street executives do on a daily basis. In championing development initiatives, especially in developing nations, the bank assumes the responsibility of creating and ensuring the sustainability of such initiatives in these countries. This means that time is not a constraint in World Bank affairs but an asset. Consequently, time should act as a means to change in instituting sustainable growth and development in countries where the World Bank channels billions of dollars.

Chapter Six

⚜

What Is a State?

*Protecting ourselves under the colonial boundaries
is simply backward and cannot help Africa as
a continent to face its own challenges.*

—Author

The terms *country*, *state*, and *nation* are often used interchangeably; however, there are differences. To better define a State, we should observe the capital "S." A State (with a capital "S") is defined as a self-governing political entity. Most of the time, a State can also mean a country. On the other hand, a nation is a tight-knit group of people who share a common culture. A nation-state is a nation that has the same borders as the state.

What Defines a State or an Independent Country?

1. It is a territory with internationally recognized boundaries.
2. It has people who live there on a daily basis.
3. There are economic activities and an organized economy to answer to the basic economic questions: What goods are to be produced? For whom should

the goods be produced? How much of the goods should be produced? And for how much should the goods be sold? That said, with an established economy, economic regulation exists so as to have an institutionalized policy framework charged with economic regulation.

4. The power of social transformation is paramount within a State or country. Such social transformations may include education, cultural integration programs, research in science and technology, and so on. Therefore, the country or state is the backbone to embracing the social issues, like cultural advancement, relationship-building with other States, etc.

5. There is a transportation system to address the needs of the State's economic activities. The transport system is not and must not be static; it is improved as the economic conditions or trends evolve.

6. A State or country is sovereign with a government that is charged with the responsibility of providing social services, for example, security, education, health care, etc., to its citizens. Further, the State also has power through the established government to control the country's territory and protect its people. Above all, the government of the day in a State or country must be determined by the people and for the people through democratic elections.

7. The established State also positions itself to gain external recognition by other countries. But territories of countries or individual parts of a country are not States in their own right. The United States as a country has amassed territories like Puerto Rico,

Guam, and the Virgin Islands, which American taxpayers have to foot the bill for sustaining in terms of social transformation.

On the other hand, a state (with a lowercase "s") is usually a division of a federal State. The states of the United States of America are an example of this category. India and China are other established countries with drawn state boundaries. The European Union (EU) is also making significant progress in trying to formalize itself into one huge country. But today, it is not one country; instead, it is a loose alliance of European nations sharing mutual benefits. The challenge with the European Union is the divergent interests posed by the individual countries, which are mainly political and economic in nature. Moreover, the EU alliance is one example African countries can decide to copy or learn from as they pursue a United States of Africa—the dream of Muammar Gaddafi, the president of Libya.

African countries can decide to dismantle the temporary colonial boundaries and embrace both economic and political integration to form one country. Protecting ourselves under the colonial boundaries is simply backward and cannot help Africa as a continent to face its own challenges. The African continent is a candidate for sustainable growth and development if its leaders decide to remove the colonial borders, embrace integration, and come out of the current backwardness of holding on to the survival of the loose "countries" that we have today.

Nations and Nation-States

Nations are naturally homogeneous groups of people larger than a single tribe or community that share a common language, institutions, religion, and historical experiences. When nations of people have a State or country of their own, they are called nation-states. Places like Egypt, Germany, and France are good examples of nation-states. There are some States that have two nations, for example Belgium and Canada. Despite its multicultural society, the United States is also referred to as a nation-state as a result of the shared American culture. Present-day African countries can integrate to form one nation-state, because most of continental Africa is linked to one common heritage. President Museveni[16] of Uganda argues that, "African peoples are linked linguistically even before we talk about other aspects of life."[17] The statement suggests that the African people can easily understand each other if they listen carefully. This is because pronunciations of most words differ, but they are still similar across most parts of the continent. Therefore, why should a mere difference in the pronunciation of words hold people captive to poverty and desperation? That is, why can't they cross borders and trade with other people? Secondly, is it possible to rule out language differences as a cause for the poor performance of the African states in global trade? Furthermore, should we then adhere to the suggestion by O'Brien and Williams[18] that the "culturalists see the cause of poverty in the continent of Africa as the behavior of the poor while the global historicists ... see it as a result of the relationship between the poor and the rich"? Consequently, it is important to suggest that the African continent use its abundant languages as potential marketing tools for goods and services in the respective subregions where the languages are spoken. But this is only possible if the colonial boundaries are removed for the sake of integration and sharing the enormous skills the African people possess. This can surely happen if a more unifying government is crowned as the African Federal Government is instituted. This hypothetical federal government of Africa must initiate "second generation reforms needed to produce an emerging society" which "will take a lot more patience and hard work."[19] The hard work includes tackling issues like developing the diverse skills and the hardworking population necessary to increase the production of goods and services with significant quality and quantity for the eventual growth and development of the continent to be realized.

Finally, there are some nations without States, including, among others, Kurdistan in Iraq, where the Kurds seem to be stateless. But the fact is that the recent U.S.-led war in Iraq has proved beyond doubt that Kurdish statehood is still a dream. Their struggles have continued despite setbacks, especially their suffering under Saddam Hussein's ruthless regime. But the fact is that for a nation to emerge in Africa, revolutionaries have to take the center stage and justly fight for the cause and dreams of the "African nation." These revolutionaries should not use guns, as those in the past have done, but rather intellect to overcome the backward mentalities.

Chapter Seven

⟨ℳ⟩

We Must Build Modern African States

Lack of money is a symptom, not a cause of poverty. Poverty is cured not with money but by gaining access to the productiveness—the skills, tools, and assets, in that order—required to earn money.
—Author

The African Diaspora: The Key to Africa's Sustainable Development

No single person or institution has a monopoly on solutions to Africa's development challenges. But "business as usual" has not helped Africa in the last forty years and is not going to help Africa in the foreseeable future, unless we change our way of thinking. We need to "think outside the box" for new ideas. A great deal of creativity and innovation is needed from Africans, both at home and abroad, as well as from friends of Africa and Africa's development partners, to tackle our multiple problems, which we must do if we are going to achieve the Millennium Development Goals (MDGs) by 2015.

Although Africa has a lot of sympathizers around the world, Africans cannot just sit back and expect to be spoon-fed by the international community forever. Neither can we afford to blame others indefinitely for our malaise. Africans, both at home and in the Diasporas must ultimately assume the greater burden of determining their destiny. Speaking as one African to another, I say we need to advance breakthrough ideas and map out viable implementation strategies for agreeable solutions to enhance the quality of life of our people, who look to us, the elite, for salvation from poverty and the misery of underdevelopment.

Poverty Reduction

The phrase *poverty reduction* has gained traction in development discourse, though many people use it deceptively in situations that contribute nothing to reducing poverty. Better roads, free education, free health care, and the elimination of corruption, the usual popular gauges of how rich or poor the citizens of a country are, are not true signs improvement. Rather, something called "per capita income," which is the average annual income of individuals in the country, is the real measure of citizens' wealth. Even if some magical donors were to enable the government to provide its citizens with better physical infrastructure as well as free education and health care and other goodies, the citizens would still be as poor as they were before the arrival of the mythical benefactor.

What is amiss? None of these freebies puts money in the individual pockets of the masses. On the other hand, if a magic wand created millions of new jobs, entrepreneurs, and *asset* owners, it would most certainly lead to a rise in the per capita income. The citizens would be better off. The tax base would expand, meaning more sustainable revenue for the government. From the taxes, the government would have more money for those roads, schools, and hospitals when corruption is a controlled variable.

How do Western countries address poverty in their own ranks? In the United States alone, there are numerous poverty alleviation programs in the government and private sectors. And there are just as many such programs in the EU countries as well. All these programs have one characteristic in common. They put real money (cold cash) in the hands of the poor, by design, to maintain aggregate consumption levels for a robust economy. Why can't the West apply their age-old proven techniques to poverty-stricken countries in the Third World? Not one such program is being promoted in Africa. Is African poverty different from Western poverty? Suffice it to say that the Heavily Indebted Poor Countries program (HIPC)[20] has been in existence since 1996 with successful implementations in a number of countries, yet no one can identify any post-HIPC countries where poverty reduction has been recorded or by how much.

People know poverty when they see it; they also know prosperity when they see it. We need an acceptable definition of poverty reduction based on standard measures that everybody can see. Nobody, not even in the World Bank, has come up with a concise definition of poverty reduction or a way to measure it. So, first things first, we need to participate in determining the definition of this concept and set parameters upon which we can all agree.

The "symptomatic economics" (i.e., the tendency to address symptoms instead of causes) arise from the school of thought that sees money as the cure for poverty or food as the solution to hunger. Lack of money is a symptom, not a cause, of poverty. Poverty is cured not with money but by gaining access to the productiveness—the skills, tools, and assets, in that order—required to earn money. There are quite a number of accidents claiming innocent people—including decision makers—in many African countries. Leaders there seem to reason that governments do not have money to construct better and sustainable road networks. The message I have for them is that they should use whatever money is available to fix the roads in a more permanent form and mobilize the masses to utilize those roads for productive means. It is pointless to have good roads with no productive means or economic strategy to use the infrastructure in place.

Migration and the African Diaspora

The African expatriates living and working in America and Europe are Africa's most precious and underutilized resource. These individuals not only earn money abroad through both petty (*kyeyos*) and professional jobs and send some of it back to their families; they also represent an incredible human resource of expertise, knowledge, education, experience, entrepreneurship, and enthusiasm that can be deployed creatively on a host of development fronts back home in Africa, if only we could create ideas with attractive incentives. I decry leaders who torment their opponents and force them into exile; these people end up adopting a different lifestyle and work ethic, and because they cannot return home for fear for their lives, they end up spending all their hard work and earned income in Western capitals. Therefore, Africa, as a continent, needs ideas that put the nationals of the country in the "driver's seat" under the premise that development is a do-it-yourself proposition. No one can develop Africa but Africans themselves.

For a long time, African leaders have been gathering in high-profile summits of their own to discuss African crises on their own terms, but no results have been apparent. Their ineffectiveness may well lie in their official neglect to engage their own people in a national dialogue. The challenge of our underdevelopment is too big to leave to the politicians alone. We, as Africans in the Diasporas, have also been conducting our own well-attended conferences in various Western capitals propounding all kinds of solutions that never see the light of day. What we do best is simply daydream of establishing entities that will never be until we step foot into those countries we call home. It's backward for us to remain in the above state of affairs, helping other countries develop while ignoring our own and yet claiming we have the best and richest culture ever to exist on Planet Earth. It is very common for Africans to "claim" to think big but have no concrete plan on the ground. Our creation is a dream. We should rise up and realize tangible benefits in Africa.

Picture of Ugandans attending the 2009 Annual Convention in Chicago, Illinois, under the umbrella of UNAA (Uganda North American Association). Such conventions help cities in the United States with revenue collection through taxes levied on room and board fees paid to the hotels to accommodate the conventions. The revenues collected by the cities, in turn help to pay the hosting city bills and promote its growth and development. There are no tangible benefits for Uganda and Africa as a whole if delegates do not transform information gathered in these conventions into practical investment opportunities.

Credit is given to Mr. Solomon W. Jagwe and Mr. Ronnie Mayanja of UNAA Times – The Ugandan's voice in the Diaspora for making this photo available

There is no point in rehearsing African problems in every forum. Who doesn't know the "anatomy of African problems"? The hard part is agreeing on solutions. Analyzing in hindsight is always easy. It is thinking ahead that is hard. The African presidents, who are the prime movers of the New Partnership for Africa's Development (NEPAD),[21] have called for a credible plan to involve the African Diasporas in NEPAD. They are right. Africans in the Diasporas are clearly underutilized. They can do a lot more if offered the right incentives. This is the community whose aggregate remittance to their home countries far exceeds all forms of foreign aid combined. Africans in the Diasporas could serve a dual function: they could act as a base for external resource mobilization and also as a lobbying group in Western capitals to promote increased inflows of foreign direct investment (FDI). It stands to reason that foreigners cannot be enticed to invest in Africa if Africans themselves are not investing there. Therefore, we should send money to our relatives, not for them to buy meat and clothes and have a good time, but to impart to them a culture of instituting homegrown investments that can increase their incomes to supplement their livelihoods. We should also utilize our relatives and friends to form links to investment opportunities in Africa where we can direct the remittances as opposed to spending it here on burgers and fries.

Remittances

Remittances stimulate the economy by increasing currency flow and consumer purchasing power. These are literally life-saving injections, but we can't help everybody in the whole country individually. Instead, when we help our countries economically through ingenious programs and the economies improve; the effects spill over to everybody in the country. We can mobilize expatriate Africans to pool their remittances to purchase one or more of the state-owned enterprises (SOEs) slated for privatization, resulting in widespread ownership of these assets by the nationals of the country and the plowing back of their dividend earnings into the economy, leading to massive economic stimulation, accelerated growth, and poverty reduction. *The members of the African Diasporas constitute the most indispensable catalyst in the accelerated development of their home countries because they have a permanent vested interest in the well-being of their people.*

Ownership Culture

There is no sustainable way to implement poverty reduction unless Africa widens the base of economic participants. When knowledgeable people speak of indigenous capital ownership as the *sine qua non* of sustainable development, they point to the right solution. There is a need for us to engage in a new and specific development paradigm, based on broad participation of the population in market-driven economic activities. If this paradigm is adopted, Africa can create millions of entrepreneurs and business asset owners and not just a handful of millionaires. The ingenuity of this concept, called Direct Expatriates Nationals Investment (DENI), is to widen the base of Africans participating in the revival and stimulation of their economies.

Initiatives, such as NEPAD, pride themselves on looking for African solutions to African problems. NEPAD has a lot of laudable goals, but they are based on the wrong premise that money is the cause of development, not the effect. The truth of the matter is the other way around. The strategy should be to impress upon African governments the need to support a privatization and commercialization model that advances broad indigenous ownership of income-generating assets and does not simply make the rich richer. Specific and transparent policy initiatives, in this regard, are likely to be more fruitful and the results more robust if all those focusing on poverty reduction insist on a steady broadening of asset ownership, which corresponds to a steady and measurable alleviation of poverty. That is the litmus test of a value-added contribution. The asset-ownership strategy, so far, has been the overlooked component in the improvement of the African continent. It holds the great promise of turning asset-less citizens into proactive stakeholders in the stability of their own continent.

People create wealth, not the government. This is a classic example of an anomaly where all the planned expenditures on government programs can be met under the MDGs and yet the people will still be poor. This is the hidden danger we see facing the MDGs in the African region. NEPAD has failed to inspire ordinary people because of its lopsided emphasis on government programs rather than on people-driven initiatives.

Development

Africa's development is linked to its ability to attract investment capital in terms of both money and skilled people, who are technologically savvy and who can develop robust private-sector economies in Africa. The challenge facing Africa is to raise the level of private investment to promote development, particularly in infrastructure and technology. But foreign direct investors (FDIs) are not going to invest in Africa if Africans themselves are not investing in their own economies. So, Africans both at home and abroad must lead the way and show that we have full confidence in our economies. This is the only reliable way to create jobs and wealth, thereby eradicating poverty. Foreign direct investment follows a modicum of development; it does not precede it.

The Debt Forgiveness Campaign spearheaded by Jubilee2000 inadvertently thwarted Africa by infusing the African leadership with the obsession that debt forgiveness is a panacea for all our development problems. It is not. And now we are learning the hard truth that the debt forgiveness that so many fought for has not resulted in poverty reduction. Thus, poverty will continue even with the cancellation of debt. Debt can be cancelled with the stroke of a pen, but poverty cannot be cancelled the same way. What is needed is a long-term self-help recovery strategy based on people-driven programs that will turn Africa from aid dependency to trade dependency. That is how all nations developed. No nation has ever developed by aid alone. History tells us that most successful nations relied on trade and commerce. Africa cannot be the exception. In chapter 10, I will expose you to the possible ways African leaders can empower their people through representation to effect change and eliminate poverty in their nations and, of course, their households.

Chapter Eight

⌒⁀⌒

Foreign Aid Has Not Been Effective in Africa

Foreign aid operates in accordance with the "flypaper effect,"
systematically generating incentives and opportunities for the
expansion of government spending.

—Remmer[22]

For a long time, African leaders have traveled and given speeches in foreign capitals, dined with the leaders of rich countries, lobbied for aid, and devised strategies for making this aid effective. But in all these travels, they end up spending the same aid or taxpayers' money with no marginal benefit because the aid they get has always failed to be effective. In a world where development is perceived to have drivers and passengers, initiating dialogue among passengers (poor countries) and drivers (developed countries) on how society can avoid potholes in the fast lane will definitely lead to disaster.

African officials should instead opt for meetings on how to get off aid (development aid) and not the other way around. The idea of running around and giving endless speeches in the Western capitals should become a thing of the past. It is backward both in action and in thinking. Poor countries are tired of being passengers; they want to drive their own economies.

The aid effectiveness initiative is geared toward sustaining poor nations in the seat of expectations. According to an eighty-year-old *mzee* (old man) in Western Kenya, Africans are poorer than they were when the majority were illiterate. Following are the words of the old *mzee* from Western Kenya: "Son, you people have education, but you cannot afford a cow to pay dowry, and even if you married, your wife has no land to till—we (educated and illiterate) all retreat to our villages and stare at each other!"

Africans stare at each other day in, day out, waiting for the next move from donors—but not Africans themselves. We simply cannot look at each other and view or imagine progress. We see each other as individuals with the same problems and thinking.

Development is not static. There is no way poor nations will catch up by simply eyeing success through the lenses of developed societies. What countries in Africa ought to be doing is focusing on learning the secrets behind the success of wealthy nations. No such secret will be revealed at the conferences our leaders attend and even address in hopes of attracting more aid. The focal point for such conferences is to basically institutionalize aid dependency.

The over $650 billion U.S. dollars (2004 prices) that has been pumped into sub-Saharan Africa for the last fifty years may have brought a highway, a hospital, an airport, and even a school among other things, but it failed to build a confident African, who would creatively utilize it to confront his daily challenges. That explains in part why African countries that boast of holding 13 percent of the world's oil reserves still import oil and refined fuel. The Democratic Republic of Congo, for example, holds an estimated 70 percent of the world's Colton (in which Tantalum is extracted) and 34 percent of its (Colton) Cassiterite (two minerals strategic in the production of cell phones, laptops, and other portable electronics), but it will still join the aid effectiveness queue. But no single cell phone in the Democratic Republic of Congo can claim to have been manufactured in that country with the use of her minerals.

Donor countries, on the other hand, have a constituency of citizens who transform problems into money-making opportunities. For instance, Africans have witnessed tremendous growth in the cell phone industry, which grows at 39 percent annually against the global growth average of 22 percent. In Kenya, the traditional fixed-line telecom started uprooting its old phone booths from the city center in late August 2004 in preparation to go wireless. African people want opportunities to make money like their counterparts in developed countries, not to be trapped in some "feel-good" aid initiatives.

Africa is rich in opportunities, but many tasks—extracting minerals from underground and adding value to them; providing quality and relevant education, health care, and sanitation; producing agricultural goods and food; and developing infrastructure, among others—must be undertaken for the opportunities to have a real chance. Billions of dollars of African potential are trapped by reliance on aid. These conferences and summits that solicit aid will further trap Africans in what Professor Gregory Clark[23] refers to as the Malthusian trap where "technological advances merely produce more people and living standards are driven down to subsistence."

By emphasizing aid effectiveness in these conferences and summits, Africans will not gain the freedom to travel the world, learn, develop, and make money. Hushed up in the big-sounding partnership objectives is the rich nations' quest to lock Africans in Africa by attempting to export the West to Africa! As Professor Gregory Clark argues in his book, *A Farewell to Alms: A Brief Economic History of the World*, a visitor to Planet Earth, who was ignorant of its history, "would see, ringing the modern West, a series of fortifications protecting it from invasion by the poor societies of South America, Africa, and South Asia." Such a visitor would witness the fears of Western societies through Paul Collier's (*The Bottom Billion*) quest to protect his son from a world with a vast, running sore—a billion people stuck in desperate conditions alongside unprecedented prosperity.

Clearly, the agendas in the conferences and summits on aid are not "owned" by poor nations, because if they were, such meetings would focus on how to make resources on continents like Africa benefit their own people. If the agenda were to be set by poor nations, they would be pushing for the opening up of commercial financial institutions to support African entrepreneurs so they could be globally competitive. In addition to addressing aid effectiveness, poor nations ought to address what causes prosperity and unleash it upon their populations.

Chapter Nine

⌒♯⌒

Africa's Age of Enlightenment Is *Now*

Africa can re-tool its development process by creating an
"African Way" development paradigm that mixes its traditional
values and the global ones.

—Y. K. Amoako

"The majority of Africans today are poorer than those who lived in the Stone Age Era," says Professor Gregory Clark. The ongoing scramble for Africa's resources by Europe, the United States, China, India, and Turkey, among others, clearly calls for Africans sobering up and seeking positive ways to make the continent a hub of business. It also calls on Africans to attain a higher level of enlightenment not later but *now* so that they can reason and set the playing field to counter those after the continent's resources.

Comparing African history to that of Europe, one can clearly see the need to initiate the continent's own age of enlightenment. Obviously, no single individual drove the European enlightenment, but historians do point out the fact that the quest to have reason as a primary source and basis for authority created a new order in Europe. According to Professor Clark, the majority of the English, as late as 1813, were in conditions no better than their ancestors in Africa. Europeans in London were "a filthy people who squatted above their own feces, stored in the basement cesspits."

European history is dotted with tribalism, ethnicity, superstition, extreme religious beliefs, and repressive kingdoms and wars, but that ought not to be an excuse for Africans to celebrate. The lesson Europe offers, however, is that the exploitation of an inquiring mind, a mind that is willing to be rebellious and give reason the power to shape the person's life is what gave birth to Europe as we know it today. Africans ought to drive their own age of enlightenment by asking such basic questions as why a continent rich in minerals and quite intelligent people should be perceived to be poorer than the rest of the world. Why must a rich continent be aid dependent? Why is it that ethnicity in Africa is perceived to be the core of conflicts on the continent? What prevents African leaders from developing a long-term vision for their own people? How can we fuse cultural beliefs and legal systems with the larger global systems in order to bring to the surface Africa's predominantly underground economy? Should Africans simply agree with Professor Clark's assertions that no real development is taking place in Africa simply because population growth outstrips economic growth and the quality of labor output in Africa is below standard? I recommend that we Africans read the pessimistic arguments of Professor Gregory Clark in his book *A Farewell to Alms* to strengthen our case for an African-driven development strategy.

To the Western world, the riots that rocked Kenya in December 2007 and early 2008 after the bungled presidential elections were a sign of retrogression. However, analyzed critically, they can be seen as a positive sign, although I believe it was political futility. Africans can no longer let their freedoms be trampled upon by dictators. In other words, when Africans protest against repressive regimes, the Western media perceives it to be a sign of retrogression. For Kenya, the post-election violence of December 2007 highlighted the fact that people in the East African region are interdependent.

Political futility in Kenya hurts Uganda, Rwanda, Burundi, Southern Sudan, Eastern Congo, and even Somalia. In other words, the cost of political futility in Africa is going up. Kenya no longer belongs to itself—a positive sign of growing regional interdependence that will eventually drive Africa to become a one-market sphere. Surely, Africa urgently needs its own age of enlightenment *now* to ensure prosperity for every African.

The "African Way" Is the Only Way

The need for a new African development philosophy exists, but when it is realized and informed by its cultural idiosyncrasies, it will make over two thousand African ethnic groups see themselves as one. It will reinforce a new level of civilization and will draw millions of Africans from so many different tribes into civilization and foster a desire among them to cooperate and work together for mutual benefits. It will also reaffirm a new idea I call the "African way" of doing things drawn from the African culture, colonial heritage, and global prosperity process.

In *China May Be Right in Africa*, Atuahene-Gima Kwaku,[24] of the China Europe International Business School, argued that Africa has to learn from the Chinese ability to mix and positively deviate from the dominant Western development orthodoxy (more economic and democratic/political) and create a unique development process like the one that has helped China emerge as a global economic superpower. Being a teacher of innovation and marketing, Atuahene-Gima is aware that the promotion of innovation creates economic and social prosperity.

The election of Barack Obama as president has cleared the way for black achievement in the United States of America. The coming of the Obama presidency has also been described across America and the world and broadcast in the news media as the breaking of racial barriers and the elimination of a status quo at the White House. The media has also attributed it to what the country has faced in the last sixteen years summing up both Bill Clinton's and George W. Bush's presidencies. Not one or two but many media broadcasts have said that the last sixteen years were marred by scandals, intrigue, and the loss of integrity in the eyes of the American people.

Cameron Duodu,[25] a veteran journalist, proposed that the then U.S. Democratic presidential candidate, Barack Obama, who has a Kenyan (African) father and a white mother, reflects Africa's need to mix its development process with its own cultural values and the global development ones. In Obama, as is expected of Africa, African culture wasn't denigrated (with all its psychological implications). His white mother skillfully allowed him to "take in all cultures with respect" in his development process. The result is Obama, who is balanced developmentally, emotionally, and intellectually. Today, many view Obama's leadership as authentic. It is authentic leadership because it has been characterized by elements like confidence, optimism, hope, resilience, strong moral character, high standards and values, and advanced cognitive and emotional processes. President Obama's leadership is also seen to be transformational, open, and inclusive. This was evidently displayed during the health-care debate. He reached out to multiple sides to seek different and balanced perspectives so that the issue was debated in a more open and transparent manner. African leaders have to embrace this very kind of leadership and incorporate their political opponents—not enemies—into the political process to get the continent out of its backwardness.

Further, Y. K. Amoako, the former chair of the UN Economic Commission for Africa, says that Africa is the only continent whose development process is dominated by foreign development paradigms to the detriment of its rich traditional values. For psychological reasons, the import of China and Obama is that Africa can retool its development process by creating an "African way" development paradigm that mixes its traditional values with global ones. Lack of a clear and detailed "African way" might have prompted City University of New York's Steve Panford to argue that Africa needs transformational elites to think out loud from within African cultural ideals for progress. But this can only be possible if African leaders have risen to the occasion to assume leadership of the "African way." For instance, in "Searching for Transformational Elites in Ghanaian Development"[26], Panford says that Ghanaian traditional values should inform Ghana's progress. Ghana prides itself on being the "Black Star of Africa," but it hasn't demonstrated any attempts at forging an "African Way."

The "Asian way" was created by Asia's transformative elites. Whether in Malaysia's Mahathir Mohammad, Japan's Akio

Morita, South Korea's General Park Chung Hee, Taiwan's General Chiang Kai-shek, Singapore's Lee Kuan Yew, or China's Deng Xiaoping, we see Panford's transformational elites as directors of progress who have a vast grasp of their cultural values and the global prosperity ideals. There is no doubt, though, that there are some rifts between tradition and Capitalism in the Asians' march to prosperity. The Asian miracle is now sometimes called "Confucian Capitalism," a reminder of their elites' ability to play with their cultural values and the neoliberal development paradigms. The result, as Robert Kagan indicates in *The Return of History and the End of Dreams*, is an "Asian arc of freedom and prosperity" stretching from Japan to Indonesia to India. Minting an "African way" doesn't mean abandoning the good parts of Africa's colonial heritage, but as Atuahene-Gima argued, Africa's progress necessitates the need to "develop systems of government that take into account the peculiarities of Africa without throwing away elements of other systems that may be useful to us."[27] Already, Botswana has shown the way, and the result is prosperity throughout the last twenty years. The time has come to tout credibly the "African way" as a development paradigm. We, as Africans, must see this paradigm and run with it.

Chapter Ten

⌐₥₋

Empowering Africans

We must start from the simple premise that
Africa's future is up to Africans.
—President Barack Obama

The last nine chapters have demonized Africans as being backward in almost everything, but chapter 10 should exonerate us from that mentality. I have dedicated this chapter to prescribing solutions to the African backward way of thinking. I focus on creating a citizenry that is empowered—with skills, reason, and wisdom. The prescriptions in this chapter are my own ideas that can be adopted or rejected by you, the readers, who might include African leaders. The ideas can also be modified and researched further for improvement or to suit one's desires. The best definition I can give to economic empowerment is the ability to achieve self-reliance by a country or an individual through reducing dependence on foreign aid or other people (for the sake of individuals) and embarking on active trade policies to support most of the nation's or person's economic development needs. Individuals in this case can embark on creative means to come out of the shadows of poverty, disease, hopelessness, and, worse still, backward mentalities. Further, how will Africans achieve individual economic empowerment? This is a question to be addressed by politicians, academicians, and policy experts. However, the more a country depends on foreign aid, the more her people will likely believe that aid is the only way out of poverty, disease, and backwardness. As individuals, we should remain in families like the Basoga culture wants us to do, but the practice of pampering aged children without guiding them to confront the future must stop. It must stop if we are to reduce our dependency syndrome and become productive human beings ready to develop our economies.

Indeed, many studies have pointed to the fact that foreign aid is likely to keep poor people even poorer with no alleviation in sight. For instance, Sanchez[28] questions the validity of foreign aid and concludes that whether aid is invested or consumed, it is hardly reflected in the indicators of human development (infant mortality, literacy levels, life expectancy, etc.). The same study adds that:

> Economic aid in its current form exists allegedly, because there are great disparities of wealth between countries. But there is no general agreement that the primary objective of aid is the development of poor countries, and in some cases aid programs are supported on the grounds that they further political and or economic interests of the aid granting countries or groups within these countries.[29]

On the other hand, Craig Burnside and David Dollar's[30] study advances the argument that "aid has a positive impact on growth in the developing countries with good fiscal, monetary, and trade policies but has little effect in the presence of poor policies." The argument offers some support for the effectiveness of aid. This study, however, points out the fact that the growth of developing nations depends to a large extent on their own economic policies whether good or bad. Studies by Paul Collier and Jan Dehn,[31] Carl-Johan Dalgaard and Henrik Hansen,[32] Patrick Guillaumont and Lisa Chauvet,[33] Henrik Hansen and Finn Tarp,[34] Robert Lensink and Howard White,[35] and Collier and Dollar[36], all extend quite varying explanations of how effective foreign aid is when applied in countries with good economic policies. Moreover, the study by William Easterly, Ross Levine, and David Roodman[37] deeply underscores the view that even with good policies; foreign aid effectiveness in recipient countries is limited and makes suggestions to economists and policy makers to use more complex methodologies in trying to understand the benefit foreign aid offers to recipient nations. Yet, since most developing nations are characterized by the presence of poor fiscal policies and especially corruption, aid seems to be of little importance to them in forging developmental goals.

The studies by Peter Boone[38] confirm that foreign aid did not raise growth rates in a typical poor country. Paul Mosley[39] suggests that citizens of donor countries are aware of the quantity of aid being sent out, but they are unable to tell what good foreign aid produces or the impact of it on the recipient countries. This reinforces the idea that tangible results from foreign aid are hardly visible in the recipient countries. Furthermore, Brumm,[40] Ovaska,[41] Remmer,[42] Sanchez, and Mosley, Hudson, and Horrell[43] conclude and offer significant results showing that indeed development aid does not contribute to the economic development of the developing nations. Most important to note here is that foreign aid operates in accordance with the "flypaper effect," systematically generating incentives and opportunities for the expansion of government spending.[44]

I have included this portion on foreign aid to put emphasis on the fact that foreign aid will never develop and empower the continent of Africa. It is critical to point out that fair-trade policies rather than foreign aid must be made the point for negotiation when African leaders attend those endless seminars and conferences in Western capitals. Fair-trade policies will provide cheaper, short-term realization of economic empowerment, which aid has failed to do for decades.

Therefore, the "premise that Africa's future is up to Africans," as boldly stated by President Obama in Accra, Ghana, on July 11, 2009, is a proclamation that roared over Africa that time around. But it is also the proclamation that African leaders least expected to come from a president of the Western world because they are used to the usual consolations and demoralizing comments on how pathetic the continent is and how necessary it is to increase aid to solving the implacable problems. The African problems, to some Western leaders, have no end in sight, but they are also critical motivators and campaign tools for support from African leaders in allowing them to plunder the continent of its rich resources and exploit the poor African minds. Therefore, President Obama's message stands to change the course and call on Africans to solve their own problems. The problems must be solved using ideas that were started by revolutionary Africans decades ago, whose messages nobody from the Western world has come to embrace. Consequently, as I conclude this book, I feel that a dialogue should be opened up for Africans, especially African leaders and the so-called intellectuals of the continent, to embark on a campaign of making the continent the beacon of success for all Africans. The task is not going to be easy, but it can be done.

It can be done if African leaders seek to effect change through modern constitutional governments; and also show willingness to effect that change first; through education of fellow-citizens to want some change. Secondly, the leaders must persuade the citizens to want the particular change they deserve.

In seeking to find ways to make Africa and Africans empowered, I am offering the following ideas for discussion in both the public and academic realms. Politicians and policy makers ought to approach the implementation of these ideas very aggressively if they want to change both the mind-sets and the conditions that have caused Africans to remain in a state of backwardness.

1. *Establishment of modern education facilities with a curriculum that is capable of addressing the developmental needs of the continent*

We saw in chapter 3 that regardless of whether Africans study abroad or on the continent, their propensity to carry that educational achievement to greater heights in developing their own countries has not been great; at the most, it has been marginally measurable. Therefore, the new education curriculum must address what can take the continent out of the backward way of thinking. To draw a line from Professor Mahmood Mamdani's interview with the *Sunday Vision*[45]:

> A country which wants to lead in anything has to seriously invest in research; otherwise, it will be forever

dependent on what others produce as knowledge. The problem with depending on other countries' knowledge is that they don't face the same problems which we face as Uganda or Africa. It is through your own research initiatives that you can think for yourself.

The curriculum created must incorporate explanation of how its objectives will address the problems of Africa or the individual African countries. It also has to address the issue of producing graduates who possess the ideas characterized by Mr. Eric Kimani[46] as "abundance mentality." The CEO of Sameer Africa (formally Firestone, East Africa) defines abundance mentality as a deep belief that there is enough for all—enough work, enough jobs, and enough resources. It is living with a favor-minded attitude. One can define it also as being optimistic about the future—that is to say, seeing the glass as half full instead of half empty. Abundance mentality is also associated with thinking big and expecting big. We Africans have a problem of making our minds barriers to our success; we are never contented in ourselves despite achieving great strides in education. We are simply associating ourselves with what Mr. Kimani calls the "scarcity mentality." This is the opposite of the abundance mentality. It is the belief that one's success implies somebody else's failure; that there are scarce resources and if you get them, you must be denying someone else; that there is a scarcity of jobs; or that the political cake is not big enough to be shared, or whoever shares in it must have some kind of favor to sacrifice to the appointing authority. This is the effect of *paternalism* in institutional development and effectiveness. This is an idea that governance means that all power flows directly from the leader. It constitutes the blending of both public and private sectors. Regimes that practice *paternalism* are sometimes referred to as autocratic or oligarchic and exclude the middle and lower classes from power. The scarcity mentality is a problem in Africa and our current education systems have not fully prescribed ways to come out of it. Developed countries are where they are today because they are associated with the abundance mentality; citizens in those countries have internal security based on principle-centered living. Their value system is self-anchored. They are not so worried about doing certain things the wrong way because they always talk from the point of truth. This frees their minds to form bigger and better thoughts because they have nothing to cover up. In respect to the above, they are risk takers. By contrast, we Africans who have a scarcity mentality are always seeking validation from our parents, spouses, friends, and the groups that influence us, you name it. We rarely want to take action on our own. We simply want others to validate us before we take any action; therefore, we are simply not risk takers. In also addressing our education curriculum, we should focus the targets on reading and comprehension. People with an abundance mentality keep their minds and bodies toned through reading and exercise. In contrast, we Africans stop reading upon graduation. The curiosity to read and be aware of our environments and politics is not on our agenda—and this explains why we die sooner than our age-mates in the developed world. Reading simply informs us of so many things, including ways to take care of our health. Psalm 118:24 says, "This is the day the Lord has made; let us rejoice and be glad in it." This verse is very profound for those who read the Bible often. If we put this verse into practice, we can avoid worrying so much about our surroundings; instead, we can be filled with joy and appreciation for each and every moment that comes by. We should like and love everything we see and do for the good of our own lives. Moreover, when we read—and read widely for that matter—we will remain relevant to ourselves and our dear continent. The education curriculum I am advocating must make us relevant and able to climb new mountains. We should not be worrying about the problems of climbing such mountains. That said, we must know our problems as a continent and devise local solutions to solve them instead of importing the solutions.

2. *The establishment of permanent physical infrastructure*
This should include roads, irrigation schemes, schools, medical facilities, and so on. Technical experts charged with these new developments must design projects that can last for a much longer time than those we have today, whether the money to be used is to come from taxpayers or development aid. The need for investment in tangible, durable, and long-lasting infrastructure has never taken precedence among African developmental experts and their policy directors. The people charged with designing our infrastructure-development plans must have some level of abundance mentality in their service. People with abundance mentality serve others. Service, according to one philosopher, "is the only rent to pay for the privilege of living in this world."[47]

3. *The freedom to make independent and informed economic decisions with less government intervention should prevail.*
This will increase creativity among the citizens as they race toward becoming entrepreneurs within their own countries. Many years ago, economists predicted that countries in which

people enjoy a large degree of economic freedom will develop and grow more quickly than those in which people experience little economic freedom. Besides rehearsing these economic theories, the need to build in ourselves the courage to do things is paramount to realizing our freedom to make independent economic decisions. Fear of the unknown should be a thing of the past; we should learn to invest our money in productive ways without any need for fear. Some of us have been made captive by the jobs we do day in and day out, and we fear quitting these jobs and finding ways of entering into others or even starting businesses. We should learn and develop the courage to do the things we have not done before, because courage is an essential attribute for great minds.

4. *Taxes and interest rates must be kept low and excellent fiscal discipline emphasized.*

Without getting into the tax policy politics of Washington DC, they are characterized by low taxes (Republican campaign tactic) and high taxes (the Democratic Party looks to be the party of higher taxes according to Republicans). Taxes in African countries need an effective and expanded base and a rather progressive tax policy to encourage inventions and innovation. We should also abandon the idea of taking advantage of the very rich to finance public programs and focus on the notion that every citizen deserves the opportunity to pay his or her share. Businesses that innovate and creative minds that focus on inventions must be encouraged through subsidies and at the least be subjected to low taxes. There is no time for African countries to engage in a debate about which people should pay low taxes and when. We must leave the debate to those who are already considered in real terms to be developed. Besides, the hypothetical inclination is that when low taxes are imposed on income (whether corporate profits or personal income), investment funds will be generated and the supply of loanable funds will increase in the economy—thereby increasing the levels of investment in a country. This is what most economists have come to agree on. The people in Africa must be encouraged to appreciate the need to pay taxes as a responsibility of good citizenship and economic advancement of their continent. It shouldn't be a debate like the one we are used to in Washington DC every election year. By paying taxes, citizens are abrogated from violating the law of the harvest—let us pay what is due of us and let us reap what we have sown in the time for harvest—these two issues should go hand in hand. As people are encouraged to honor their obligations as citizens, governments must also exercise their duties by presiding over fiscally responsible money management policies. Most African nations today do not use money coming out of their own resources (i.e., taxing citizens or national investments), but that coming from the resources of other countries, especially the West, in the form of foreign aid. Whether governments are spending taxpayers' money or foreign aid, fiscal responsibility must prevail. Corruption and other forms of fiscal immorality must be curtailed for the good of the African continent.

5. *There should be a degree of government order in terms of established democratic institutions that can facilitate economic activities in the country.*

These institutions must be independent in order to make decisions that are fair to all citizens. The decisions must be people-centered and come from the people themselves. This is because, according to George Borst, CEO of Toyota Financial Services, "When they are participating in the solution, they feel better about themselves and about their contribution. If we as leaders can motivate and coach people to make discretionary contributions, we'll get to better solutions of our problems much faster."[48] It is also important to note that, as Rob Goffee and Gareth Jones said, "Leadership is not something you do to other people. Rather you do it with others."[49] The institutions must also work within the abundance perspective whereby they value strengths and leverage resources, generating outcomes that are disproportionate to the resources with which they are working. The difference between creating the positive and eliminating the negative is subtle but potentially effective and has important implications for organizational development (Alfred, et al., 2009)[50] In addition, these organizations must operate within the confines of at least five characteristics that are essential for an organizational structure to work in today's panorama:

- The structure must provide staff with an *opportunity to learn and grow*, or they will lose interest and disengage from the institution;
- Staff must have appropriate *skills and knowledge* if they are to perform effectively;
- *Owners* need to be in place throughout the organization with the responsibility of ensuring that people deliver results, or staff will lose sight of their contribution to the goals of the organization;
- The institution must align its *infrastructure*—systems, processes, and technology—with the formal structure in order to perform effectively; and

- The institution must develop and use the right *metrics* to assess performance if the structure is to deliver the best results.[51]

Overall, government institutions in Africa today operate based on systematic complexities whose foundations are grounded in corruption and patronage and a strong executive dominance of each and every state affair. Most if not all African people have resigned themselves to the above idea even when given the opportunity to change governments at the ballot box. But changing governments may not solve any of the problems, because, as the African proverb says, "The old broom knows all corners," meaning that changing leaders to elect new ones may instead worsen the problem. In the end, we Africans have always resorted to settling with the status quo. This kind of fear and reasoning should be placed in the past, and we must desist from it. But let our leaders also concur with Marianne Williamson's[52] suggestion that:

> Our deepest fear is not that we are inadequate. Our deepest fear is that we are powerful beyond measure. It is our light not our darkness that most frightens us. We ask ourselves who am I to be brilliant, gorgeous, talented, fabulous? Actually who are you not to be? You are a child of God. Your playing small does not serve the world. There is nothing enlightened about shrinking so that other people won't feel insecure around you. We are all meant to shine as children do. We were born to make manifest the glory of God that is within us. It is not just in some of us; it is in everyone. And as we let our own light shine, we unconsciously give other people permission to do the same. As we are liberated from our own fear, our presence automatically liberates others.

Therefore, to the African leaders, get rid of the fear of vacating those offices. You are today's light, but tomorrow needs more of that bright light, which those under your leadership must deliver. The young leaders are looking up to you to act in an exemplary way and hand over the mantles of leadership; this is what those democratic institutions you have set up or are about to set up must mean for the young leaders of tomorrow. These democratic institutions in their own right represent change in the lives and deeds of the African people. African leaders must work with the African people to invoke the change that comes with these institutions. Consequently, leaders must invoke change in the institutions created in order to build trust among the populations. Robert Galford and Anne Siebold Drapeau, coauthors of *The Trusted Leader*, reduce the quality of trust leaders must show to a simple model formulated as follows[53]:

$$\text{Trust} = \frac{C + R + I}{S-I}$$

Where: C = credibility
         R = reliability
         I = intimacy
         S-I = self-interest

What this model means is that trust in leaders is heightened when followers, colleagues, and clients believe the leaders know what they are doing and talking about. Trust is also elevated when leaders apply knowledge and are technically capable of establishing a feeling within others of their credibility. Furthermore, trust is built on the premise that the leaders are judged on their track records (i.e., they must consistently be doing what they said they would). Finally, the element, *intimacy*, when removed from all the other convoluted connotations, describes the "feeling of warmth and closeness" between the leaders and their followers. It is clear that trust goes up when people are dealing with someone who is not cool, distant, and aloof, but who is inclusive, approachable, and warm.

6. *Property ownership must be made a right, not a privilege, and should be regulated to encourage innovation and invention by the citizens of a country.*

Useful property structure systems refer to laws, rules, and regulations that define rights for the use and transfer of resources. Most African countries simply have not designed or even regulated useful property structure systems, and in the recent past, many of the countries in East Africa have been grumbling about land ownership bills in both the public and legislative debates. Land ownership should not be the only focus for individuals and corporations, but government must set up incentives to reward invention and innovation. Creative minds that invent must be protected by the rule of law.

About the Author

Professor Michael D. Kaluya was born and raised in Uganda, East Africa. He attended Mwiri Primary School and Namalemba Boarding Mixed Primary School for his elementary education. He went to Busoga College Mwiri for an ordinary level certificate of education (high school diploma) and Makerere High School for his advanced level certificate of education (A-level). He moved to the United States of America in 1998 to further his education. He attended Dallas Baptist University for his bachelor of business administration and economics (May 2001) and a master of business administration in international business and economics (May 2004). He also attended the University of Texas at Dallas where he earned two additional masters: a master of science in international political economy (December 2008) and a master of arts in political science (May 2010). He is currently pursuing a PhD in business administration at Northcentral University, where he is studying institutional effectiveness, public policy and administration. Finally, Professor Kaluya is an adjunct at Cedar Valley College, Lancaster, Texas; where he teaches economics, business, and management.

The author is very grateful for the generous support of RMJ Business Solutions LLC in meeting costs toward the publication of this book.

For your Income Tax Preparation and Training|Business Consultations|Financial Planning|Moneygram|Events Organizing|Airline Travel|Hotel Bookings|Career Guidance & Notary Services

Contact them at:
732 W. Hurst Blvd, Suite 112, Hurst, TX 76053;
Tel: 817-280-9774: Fax: 817-280-9719;
E-mail: rmjbsolutions@sbcglobal.net

Notes

1 Daniel Shorr, in the article "Lessons from the fall of the Berlin Wall." Mr. Shorr was a senior news analyst for National Public Radio (NPR) in the United States and a veteran Washington journalist who broke major stories at home and abroad during the Cold War and Watergate. He died at the age of ninety-three in July 2010.

2 Thomas L. Friedman, *The Lexus and the Olive Tree* (New York: Farrar, Straus, and Giroux, LLC, 2000).

3 Lao-Tzu is traditionally regarded as the founder of Taoism and is closely associated in this context with "original", or "primordial", Taoism. Lao-Tzu received imperial recognition as a divinity in the mid-2nd century BCE. Taoism gained official status in China during the Tang Dynasty, whose emperors claimed Lao-Tzu as their relative.

4 Simon J. Nkanda, *The Monarch's Dream: Chief Manana's Wake-up Call to Africa* (Pittsburgh, PA: Dorrance Publishing Co., Inc., 2003).

5 Ibid., 35.

6 Deanna Caputo, David Dunning. What you don't know: The role played by errors of omission in imperfect **self**-assessments. *Journal of Experimental Social Psychology, Volume 41, Issue 5*, September 2005, Pages 488-505

7   Alexis de Tocqueville, *Democracy in America*, vol. 1, ed. Harvey C. Mansfield and Delba Winthrop (Chicago: The University of Chicago Press, 2000), 407.

8   Mr. Kalyegira is a columnist with the *Daily Monitor* paper of Uganda, www.monitor.co.ug.

9   In analyzing the obstacles to democratization in post-independence Africa, Mahmood Mamdani offers a bold, insightful account of colonialism's legacy--a bifurcated power that mediated racial domination through tribally organized local authorities, reproducing racial identity in citizens and ethnic identity in subjects. This is illustrated in his book: Citizen and subject: contemporary Africa and the legacy of late colonialism

10 Bishop David Oyedepo is the presiding bishop of Living Faith Church Worldwide Incorporated, which is a nearly three-decade-old ministry, made up of a church network with branches all over Nigeria and most nations of Africa. A Nigerian-based faith teacher, Bishop Oyedepo is also the founding pastor of the Faith Tabernacle, reputed to be the largest church facility in the world, seating over fifty thousand people. It is located in Lagos, Nigeria. He is also the chancellor of Covenant University, a Christian-based private university, which was established in 2002. He founded the Word of Faith Bible Institute, which is the main thrust of the church's mission activities. Please see the article at http://www.sundayvision.co.ug/detail.php?main NewsCategoryId=7&newsCategoryId=128&newsId=728762 for additional inferences on the bishop's ideas on time management in a lecture delivered in Kampala in August 2010.

11 *New Vision*, August 7, 2006. The *New Vision* is a leading Ugandan government newspaper; the article in this reference is located at http://www.newvision.co.ug/D/8/220/513780.

12 Ibid.

13 Robert Hunter Wade, "What Strategies Are Viable for Developing Countries Today? The World Trade Organization and the Shrinking of 'Development Space,'" *Review of International Political Economy*, 10, no. 4 (2003): 621–644.

14 Prince Charles Dickson is a Nigeria writer whose articles often appear on www. ChatAfrikArticles.com

15 Kenneth John Galbraith, *The Economics of Innocent Fraud: Truth for Our Time* (New York: Houghton Mifflin Company, 2004), 19.

16 Yoweri K. Museveni, "African Heritages Are Linked," *Sunday Vision*, November 4, 2007.

17 *Sunday Vision*, November 4, 2007.

18 Robert O'Brien and Marc Williams, *Global Political Economy: Evolution and Dynamics* (New York: Palgrave Macmillan Ltd., 2004).

19 Thomas Friedman, *The Lexus and the Olive Tree: Understanding Globalization* (New York: Anchor Books., 2000).

20 The HIPC program was initiated by the International Monetary Fund and the World Bank in 1996, following extensive lobbying by NGOs and other bodies. It provides debt relief and low-interest loans to reduce external debt repayments to sustainable levels. Assistance is conditional on the national governments of these countries meeting a range of economic management and performance targets. The HIPC program identified forty-two countries, thirty-two of which are in Sub-Saharan Africa, as being potentially eligible to receive debt relief (2004). These countries include: Afghanistan, Benin, Bolivia, Burkina Faso, Cameroon, Central African Republic, Chad*, Republic of the Congo, Democratic Republic of the Congo, Comoros*, Côte

d'Ivoire*, Ethiopia, Gambia, Ghana, Guinea*, Guinea-Bissau*, Guyana, Haiti, Honduras, Liberia, Madagascar, Malawi, Mali, Mauritania, Mozambique, Nicaragua, Niger, Rwanda, São Tomé and Príncipe, Senegal, Sierra Leone, Tanzania, Togo*, Uganda, Zambia. (*) indicates the seven countries yet to reach completion point for the HIPC program, and therefore entitled only to partial debt relief. The remaining 24 countries have completed the program and had their external debt cancelled in full.

21 The New Partnership for Africa's Development (NEPAD) is a program of the African Union created by Africans for Africans and implemented by Africans.

The NEPAD was adopted at the thirty-seventh session of the Assembly of Heads of State and Government in July 2001 in Lusaka, Zambia. It is meant to develop values and monitor their implementation within the framework of the African Union.

NEPAD is a merger of the Millennium Partnership for the African Recovery Program (MAP) and the OMEGA Plan. The merger was finalized on July 3, 2001. Out of the merger, NAI was born. NAI was approved by the OAU Summit of Heads of State and Government on July 11, 2001. The plan was endorsed by the leaders of the G8 countries on July 20, 2001. The policy framework was finalized by the Heads of State Implementation Committee (HSIC) on October 23, 2001, and NEPAD was formed.

What is NEPAD?

- NEPAD is a vision and program of action for the redevelopment of the African continent.
- NEPAD is a plan that was conceived and developed by African leaders.

- NEPAD is a comprehensive integrated development plan that addresses key social, economic, and political priorities in a coherent and balanced manner.
- NEPAD is a commitment that African leaders are making to the African people and to the international community to place Africa on a path of sustainable growth.
- NEPAD is a commitment African leaders are making to accelerate the integration of the African continent into the global economy.
- NEPAD is a framework for a new partnership with the rest of the world.
- NEPAD is a call to the rest of the world to partner with Africa in her own development on the basis of her own agenda and program of action.

Goals

- To promote accelerated growth and sustainable development
- To eradicate widespread and severe poverty
- To halt the marginalization of Africa in the globalization process.

For more information, see **http://www.nepad.org.**

22 Remmer, Karen L. (2004). "Does Foreign Aid Promote the Expansion of Government?" *American Journal of Political Science, Vol. 48* (1): pp. 77-92.

23 Professor Gregory Clark is a professor of economics at the University of California, Davis, and author of *A Farewell to Alms.*

24 Atuahene-Gima Kwaku is a professor of marketing and innovation management and director of the center of

marketing and innovation at China Europe International Business School.

25 Cameron Duodu is Ghanaian born and educated. He is a journalist and author. He has worked for such media outlets as the *Guardian*, the *Observer*, the BBC, the *Financial Times*, the *Economist*, the *Sunday Times*, and *De Volkskrant* (Amsterdam) among others.

26 Kofi Akosah-Sarpong is the author of Transformational Elites and Ghana's Development quoted by Steve Panford of New York City. The article is published at: http://www.modernghana.com/news/150378/1/transformational-elites-and-ghanas-development.html

27 In the article Culture and Development: Promoting the African Way. A commentary by Kofi Akosah-Sarpong, Ottawa; published at http://www.thepatrioticvanguard.com/article.php3?id_article=2893

28 Omer Sanchez, "The Impact of Foreign Aid in Latin America," *Journal of Political and Economic Studies*, 27, no. 1 (2002): 22–23.

29 Ibid., 23.

30 Craig Burnside and David Dollar, "Aid, Policies, and Growth," *American Economic Review*, 90, no. 4 (2000): 847–68.

31 Paul Collier and Jan Dehn, "Aid, Shocks, and Growth," *World Bank (Washington DC) Working Paper No. 2688* (2001).

32 Carl-Jahan Dalgaard and Henrik Hansen, "On Aid, Growth and Good Policies," *Journal of Development Studies*, 37 no. 6 (2001): 17–41.

33 Patrick Guillaumont and Lisa Chauvet, "Aid and Performance: A Reassessment," *Journal of Development Studies*, 37 no. 6 (2001): 66–92.

34 Henrik Hansen and Finn Tarp, "Aid Effectiveness Disputed," *Journal of International Development*, 12 no. 3 (2000): 375–98.

35 Robert Lensink and Howard White, "Are There Negative Returns to Aid?" *Journal of Development Studies*, 37 no. 6 (2001): 42–65.

36 Paul Collier, David Dollar. (2002). Aid allocation and poverty reduction. *European Economic Review, Volume 46, Issue 8*, Pages 1475-1500.

37 William Easterly, Ross Levine, and David Roodman, "Aid, Policies, and Growth: Comment," *The American Economic Review*, 94 no. 3 (2004): 774–780.

38 Peter Boone, "Aid and Growth," Mimeo, *London School of Economics* (1994).

_____. "Politics and Effectiveness of Foreign Aid," *European Economic Review*, 40 no. 2 (1996): 289–329.

39 Paul Mosley, "The Political Economy of Foreign Aid: A Model of the Market for a Public Good," *Economic Development and Cultural Change*, 33, no. 2 (1985): 373–393.

40 Harold J. Brumm, "Aid, Policies, and Growth: Bauer was Right," *CATO Journal*, 23 no. 2 (2003): 167–174.

41 Tomi Ovaska, "The Failure of Development Aid," *CATO Journal*, 23 no. 2 (2003): 175–188.

42 Karen L. Remmer, "Does Foreign Aid Promote the Expansion of Government?" *American Journal of Political Science*, 48 no. 1 (2004): 77–92.

43 Paul Mosley, John Hudson, and Sara Horrell, "Aid, the Public Sector and the Market in Less Developed Countries," *Economic Journal*, 97 no. 387 (1987): 616–41.

44 Remmer (2004), 77.

45 *Sunday Vision*, August 26, 2010. Professor Muhmood Mamdani is now executive director for the Makerere University Institute of Social Research. Contents of his interview are available at http://www.sundayvision.co.ug/detail.php?mainNewsCategoryId=7&newsCategoryId=130...

46 Mr. Eric Kimani worked with Williamson Tea as the financial controller before he moved to KTDA to be the managing director. He is currently the CEO of Sameer Africa (formally Firestone, EA). He is the author and deliverer of the speech "The Abundance Versus the Scarcity Mentality in Professional Development and Growth," which was delivered to the Kenya Institute of Bankers, Mombasa Chapter, on December 1, 2006.

47 N. Eldon Tanner is a teacher as quoted by Brian Johnson on http://www.philosophersnotes.com/quotes/by_teacher/N.%20Eldon%20Tanner

48 Borst, G. (2009). Authentic Leadership. *Leadership Excellence, Vol. 26, Issue 1: pp. 19 - 20*

49 Goffee, R.; & Jones, G. (2009) Authentic Leadership: Excite others to exceptional performance. Leadership Excellence, July Issue 17.

50 Alfred, Richard, Shults, Chrisopher, Jaquette, Ozan, and Strickland, Shelley (2009). *Community Colleges on the Horizon: Challenge, Choice, or Abundance*, Latham, MD: Rowman and Littlefield Publishers.

51 Ibid.

52 Marianne Williamson is a spiritual activist, author, lecturer, and founder of the Peace Alliance. She is also the founder of Project Angel Food, a meals-on-wheels program that serves homebound people with AIDS in the Los Angeles

area. She has published nine books, including four *New York Times* bestsellers.

53 Co-authors Robert Galford and Anne Seibold Drapeau of *The Trusted Leader*. In Zenger, J. H., & Edinger, S. (2009). Challenging Times Demand Inspiring Leadership. *Financial Executive, July/August Issue.* www.financialexecutives.org